CHARACTER

in Georgia

by

Aka Morchilaaze

with

Peter Nasmyth

translated by
Maya Kiasashvili

MTA PUBLICATIONS
LONDON

CHARACTER
in Georgia

Published by

Mta Publications,
27 Old Gloucester St
LONDON.
WC1N 3AX
www.mtapublications.co.uk

Original publication in Georgian
'Georgian Notebook,' (2014)
Sulakauri Publishing, Tbilisi, Georgia
www.sulakauri.ge
Original Georgian text © Aka Morchiladze (2014)
Translated English text © Aka Morchiladze and Peter Nasmyth (2022)

ISBN 978-0-9559145-3-9

With thanks to the
Writers' House
of Georgia

for facilitating Maya Kiasashvili's translation work

CONTENTS

The Rikhe district of Tbilisi in the late 19th century with its floating, water powered mills. Then the city was mostly referred to by its Turkish/Persian name Tiflis. This is a good example of how much the urban landscape has since changed - as the residential district of Rikhe is now completely gone. The Soviets destroyed it when they came to build up the riverbanks. The uppermost the church was also pulled down in 1937, along with a good many others.

FOREWORD
to the original Georgian Notebook

There was a period in my life when I spent my time reading about events happening over a hundred years ago. This book is what clung on in my mind from that period. And while some events might lack ruthless accuracy, they stand out as impressions or essences – which are their main purpose. For held within them is an emerging shape – where the core of incidents and anecdotes matter most. So I never bothered reworking them. The following is what remained, lodged solidly in the heart.

Aka Morchiladze

INTRODUCTION
to the new English edition

This book started life in 2014, as the publication in Tbilisi of Aka Morchiladze's popular *Georgian Notebook*. A purely Georgian publication, written for Georgians in the Georgian language. As readers will see here, it amounts to a cornucopia of wonderful stories, anecdotes, unusual facts about key Georgians in a key period – covering the 19th and early 20th centuries. But to the outsider it is more than this. These superbly researched events, eccentricities, wicked verbal ripostes paint a larger picture – of a general character, with traits common to all. Because they are so well-chosen, one might even use that phrase, a 'national character.' For a good part of this is still the character we see today.

Which is what this new edition pursues, tries its best to spotlight. For national characters are important. They help explain why similar peoples react so differently to similar events. Also how nations follow their own unique modes of behaviour, over decades, if not centuries. And the expression of character is essential for Georgians. They love the dramatic gesture, bold acts of generosity and/or confrontation, as an essential cement for the individual Caucasian identity. Indeed it is usually said, if an action is carried out with 'heart' (*guli* in Georgian), it can be forgiven, even if wrong. Which throws the door pleasantly wide open.

The inquiry here begins by digging down into its roots. It takes the book's original text, steps back, sketches in the surrounding scenery, adds the historical and cultural background to the events.

In the original edition Aka launches straight into his stories without explanation – as most Georgian readers already know exactly who, say, 'Ilia' is. Many even know who one of his main characters, 'Luarsab' is too – they were taught Ilia Chavchavadze's famous short story about rotten nobility, *Is He a Human?* at school. Now, in this edition, more information and context is placed around the events, packing-out the stories for the non-Georgian reader, setting them more fully into the landscape out of which they grew.

Many of the first paragraphs and inserts here are written by the non-Georgian Editor. Also a good number of facts and asides have been dropped in. In the end it was decided, rather than constantly having to distinguish between Aka and the Editor's voice, the text would be melded together as one. As if written by a single person, or one might say, a joint, Anglo-Georgian being – who we hope is a human. Aka was gracious enough to allow this slightly novel approach to the original text. So it was decided to put both authors' names on the cover.

But as Aka is also a novelist himself – explaining why these stories are so elegantly described – maybe this is the natural approach anyway. In his original Foreword (above) he mentions he wrote this book mostly from memory, instinctively, like a novelist might construct a plot – except of course all the stories are true. Or at least as true as recorded history allows – sometimes harshly described as 'one person's set of opinions about something that happened'. The idea here is to give a piece of non-fiction all the detailed colour, flair, inner-rumination usually reserved for fiction.

And along the way it allows other, more interesting questions to surface, as if from a personal history. For instance, what is it that allowed the Georgian nation to so-well survive more conquests and subjugations than almost any other? What are the secret codes behind that well-known 'Georgian hospitality,' which sets out to make its enemy into its friend?

Then there's that remote, impoverished region of Guria, since labelled 'the Nazareth of Socialism.' How come in the Revolutionary period of the early 20th century, Georgia chose the more liberal, Menshevik version of Marxism, while its large northern neighbour plumped for Bolshevism? It raises the question - what makes the same nation give birth to two completely opposing types of Head of State - Noe Jordania (leader of the world's first Social Democratic nation), and the dictator Joseph Stalin?

These pages point to unexpected answers, like one hiding away in the Gurian forests - the *pirali*. Often good men, forced by the injustices of poverty into the outlaw tradition – which is unusually strong in Georgia. A kind of people's police force dispensing natural justice

INTRODUCTION

- who gradually turned themselves into revolutionaries, often violent, then formed the unique, but brief, Gurian Republic around 1905. An egalitarian, communally-run forerunner of the famous Social Democratic Georgian Republic from 1918-21.

At the same time, underlying all these characteristics is Georgia's oriental background – as epitomised by its mosques, carpets and as we shall see, the Ottoman couch. When set beside its Christian Orthodox Church and beloved sacrament of wine, it begs the old question - on what side of this half-Asian, half-European character does the Georgian heart lie?

And here Aka spotlights the issue well, by including the European traditions of opera and theatre which arrived into Georgia's late 18th century, to be taken up with a passion that survives to this day.

When considering these questions, thoughts inevitably turn to Georgia's geographical location, with its ever-present, soaring, white peaks and glaciers – whose tops are visible from most parts of the country. With every glance up comes reminders of the frequent landslides, avalanches, sudden calamities - and the Sublime. A clue perhaps why poets also play a key role in this book. Writers like Vazha Pshavela, who rejected the comfortable, lowland life to return and live up in the high Caucasus of his childhood, then proceeded to describe the mountain animism and violent blood allegiances, existing in the high villages for centuries. A man who writes a whole poem about the argument between racing river water and its stones. Who is intensely aware the huge contrasts in his country - the fierce heat of summer, the eternal deep freeze of its mountains, like Kazbek, visible from the capital. Perhaps he already sensed what has since been revealed – that Georgia is the most landscape-diverse nation for its size, in the world.

These carefully chosen stories show an instinctive awareness of this. They make sure we have chapters devoted to most of Georgia's greatest and most colourful personalities who belong to this landscape. Like the highly influential writer, banker, essayist Ilia Chavchavadze; the duel-loving prankster and Romantic poet, Nikoloz Baratashvili; the mysteriously disappearing translator of Shakespeare, Ivane Machabeli; the obsessive-compulsive children's writer and Georgian language campaigner, Iakob Gogibashvili. Some well-known people have not been included, only because the focus of this book is the pursuit of character

4

rather than delivering a full compendium of people and events. For this we ask forgiveness.

Some attempts at free-translations of Georgian poetry have also been added, to help probe deeper. Hopefully Georgian readers will see these as simply noble attempts – for as the poet Robert Frost put it - the only thing you lose when translating poetry, is the poetry. We went for inner meaning rather than strict verbal accuracy.

This book is full of names and places. Sometimes slightly bewilderingly to the non-Georgian. To help distinguish between the many similar family names, and/or nicknames from different generations, we have provided an index at the end.

And in this context a huge debt must also be conveyed to our translator, Maya Kiasashvili, whose skills she inherited from her father Niko, a well-known Shakespeare scholar who along with herself, made the first translation of James Joyce's *Ulysses*. This book is very much a joint production.

It is hoped the following pages do something to convey into English the warm, eye-for-character voice of their original author, which made *Georgian Notebook* so popular in Georgia. Aka himself kindly watched his book's slow transformation into another tongue with its many additions; dropping a few gentle hints along the way, no doubt with fingers tightly crossed that some of his original tone survives. And hopefully more than a trace of it does; that we present here a deeper than usual portrait of his always-memorable, drama-loving, character of a country.

Peter Nasmyth - *October 2022*

Chapter 1

The End of Nobility

The latter period of Georgia's nobility, just before Russia's 1801 arrival in Georgia, is an excellent place to start tracking the roots of the Georgian character we see today. For although some time ago, it's there in the relative ease of noble life that many of its cherished eccentricities are preserved. The kind that passes on invisibly up through the generations, into the faces walking our 21st century streets. And Georgia is a country of an unusually large number of noble lineages – and proud eccentricities.

When first casting one's thoughts toward that upper-strata of Georgian society in those Persian/Ottoman influenced days, a number of objects spring to mind. A sword, a *khanjali* (dagger) a flintlock, several hawks, half a dozen good horses, some hunting dogs, the throne of the country, even the King himself - for whom Georgians often sacrificed their lives - and often didn't.

But it is the low-slung divan, sometimes called the Ottoman couch, that must take pride of place. Examples are plentiful of this cherished piece of furniture - and still are. But perhaps the best doesn't require the presence of any real noblemen. One character out of Georgian fiction, does the job par excellence. Prince Luarsab Tatkaridze, from the story *Is He a Human?* by Ilia Chavchavadze (1837-1907), is often held up as a potent archetype of Georgia's former nobility, in its pre-Russian days.

So let's go straight there, to Luarsab lazing on his fictitious bench. Because the fact of his non-existence definitely helps. It makes him and his couch the perfect empty vessels to be filled with many of the old nobility's most defining traits.

While certainly there were no shortage of worse real Princes than Luarsab, this character famous for bullying his servants and thinking only of his next meal, was created by the highly influential and popular 19th

CHARACTER in Georgia

/20th century writer (Tbilisi's second largest street is named after him). Ironically Luarsab shares a few characteristics with the author himself. Both are well known for reclining on Ottoman benches, pipe in mouth, Turkish kaftan draped over their shoulders (effectively a 'smoking jacket').

This style of self-presentation had been passed down through Georgia's many oriental generations (mostly Persian and Ottoman), before the Russians arrived. Ilia's father-in-law, Prince Tadeoz Guramishvili, is well known for precisely the same style of contemplative relaxation. One eyewitness reports seeing the Prince, a man of unforgettably long moustache, reclining on the bench at the far end of a room, holding a no less unforgettably long pipe. When the mood for a smoke arrived, he'd shout across the room, 'Light it boy!' and the servant would rush in, do just that.

Similar scenes would be seen in western Georgia where another Prince - Rostom Tsereteli, father of the much-lauded writer and Ilia's friend, Akaki Tsereteli (1840-1915) - also shamelessly indulged the Ottoman bench.

One reason for this frequent horizontalism in those days, is that during peaceful times, the nobility had very little actually to do. The bench became a popular place for hours of endless dreaming about the future, discussing the fineries of the next meal or hunting trip.

Yet to be fair, being idle never sat easily with Georgian nobility. Because even while reclining there were jobs to do – like running the house and property. But without a war or imminent hunting party, the aristocracy could sometimes feel themselves held in a state of genuine, divan-boredom.

During quieter feudal periods, this may even have been order of the day. Indeed another classical writer, Grigol Orbeliani (1804-1883), in letters to his brothers, chastises his fellow aristocrats for their dependence on hawks and horses, exhorting them toward their much needed replacement - education.

And Georgian nobility did learn a few things - although mostly later. Initially the chore of education wasn't considered right for their kind. Ilia's fictitious Luarsab declared that life for any Georgian took a considerable turn for the worse at the introduction of those hellish, mind-bending institutions – colleges.

Prince Rostom Tsereteli

Fundamentally education wasn't for the nobility. Their main life-calling was being noble; or at least giving that impression.

During his lifetime Rostom Tsereteli read only two books: the *New Testament* and *The Knight in the Panther Skin* - the medieval epic by Shota Rustaveli. While copies existed in every noble household - of necessity - shelves invariably carried other publications, mainly translations from Persian literature (more often in Eastern Georgia). But all too often gathering dust. Though it might be noted that women in noble families often read more than the men.

Probably one should temper such generalisations, or the reader might think most of Georgia's nobility shunned learning. Not true at all.

CHARACTER in Georgia

Among them were several highly accomplished scholars. For instance Prince David Orbeliani, chief of Georgia's armed forces, translated the epic *Karamaniani* from the Persian. And most of the country's best poets, orators, politicians, military strategists grew out of the nobility. But given half the chance, the majority would join Luarsab on the couch, indulging their traditional, cosseted existence.

However as the 19th century rapidly loomed, so did the end of this quasi-real lifestyle; and with a certain inevitability.

When the Russian army arrived in 1801 - to add Georgia to their Empire and protect it from the all-too-frequently invading Persians - they encountered this same culture of reclining, especially in those close to the royal court and gentry. And weren't greatly impressed. It wasn't long before the local aristocracy found themselves facing significant changes; some pleasant but mostly unpleasant. The pleasant would come as lavish gifts and inventions from across the Russian Empire and Europe; the latter as a new regime of heartless obedience and financial punishment for not fitting into the brave new Northern world.

One could even elevate the metaphor - saying that what Russia encountered in Georgia's ruling class was Rostom Tsereteli's moustache. For it might be said, the weight of a nobleman's moustache then, offered more credibility in business, than any formal agreement. For inside it resided the full weight of ancestral honour. So these benighted whiskers became a symbol of personal dignity and integrity. And these qualities were supposed to be the living backbone of nobility.

For example, Akaki Tsereteli recalls an episode involving his father and a group of French businessmen visiting the Tsereteli estate. Drawn by reports of manganese in the Chiatura region, they expressed strong interests in the Prince's mineral-rich hectares. Rostom welcomed them warmly, laid out the full gamut of traditional Georgian hospitality. But when time came to formalise the agreement papers, the Prince flatly refused to sign anything. He said he considered the act of putting pen on paper crude and unnecessary; an offence to his already expressed commitment as a nobleman.

Later he told his son that he ostentatiously brushed his moustache after verbally consenting to the contract – to him a far stronger confirmation of agreement than any banal scratching of words across paper or parchment.

Shah Abbas, famous for his violent invasion of Georgia and moustache

For too long it seemed to the Russians, Georgia was a land ruled by the laws and rites of ancestral chivalry, as maintained by the nobility. So with their arrival, the inevitable shift in culture began – toward a more European, written rule of law.

Another good example of this noble behaviour came in the form of Prince Alexandre Jambakur-Orbeliani (1802-1869), leader of the failed 1832 plot against the new Russian regime. Many nobles, in fact Georgians in general, were not happy with the conditions imposed by their latest set of northern overlords.

It should be noted Alexandre's attitude towards his homeland was always highly romantic - more so than most of his contemporaries. Indeed by the end of the 1860s it could be argued there were precious few left like Prince Alexandre in all Georgia - both in opinion and appearance.

CHARACTER in Georgia

A good route into his world-view comes via snapshots of daily life in his family home. The eye might zero-in on a scene between an old man in his mid-sixties, and his four/five-year old granddaughter Mariam.

Grandfather would be set grandly upon his felt-covered Ottoman divan, surrounded by a house full of modern European style furniture. His presence on that bench was frequent, and his physical position, one of three. Horizontal, when it served as a bed. Upright with his feet on the floor, when talking to friends and relatives. Sitting cross-legged, oriental style, when writing. In this last phase, balanced on the divan beside him would often be a small three-legged table, used as a desk. His love of writing was perhaps untypical, but it certainly helps our understanding of him. And he wrote religiously every day.

Behind the bench stood a cupboard with its papers arranged in careful order. Blank sheets on the lower shelf; unfinished drafts on the middle; completed writings on the top. He would write in pencil on the tabletop, and didn't like to be disturbed.

Meanwhile his granddaughter Mariam would often sneak into the room, either to play quietly in the orbit of this stately presence, or just stand watching the old man writing. But if during play, her dolls began answering back too loudly, grandpa would softly reprimand her for interfering with his thoughts. If this didn't work, or she forgot to obey, he'd threaten to call 'Arapana' to take her away.

As for Arapana – here is another vital part of the household. A Lezgin from the North Caucasus, she'd been trusted to care for the little girl while the Prince raised and educated her. Arapana wasn't her real name, but the old man enjoyed renaming those close to him, as a gesture of affection. She arrived in the house during Russia's early 19th century war in the North Caucasus against the Islamic Imam and insurrection-leader, Shamil. After a skirmish, Russian soldiers had discovered the girl hiding parentless, inside a fireplace. To save her they took her back with them to Kvareli in eastern Georgia.

Having learned that the girl's entire family had been wiped out, the Prince and his wife took pity on her and transported her back with them to Tbilisi. After some years, the Lezgin girl's uncle finally tracked her down and asked to take her back across the mountains to her homeland. But Arapana refused, preferring to stay with the Orbeliani family.

CHAPTER 1

One could see why. The family she entered was filled with this ancient sense of trust and integrity – strengthened by the long list of hardships experienced by his particular branch of the aristocracy – due mainly to the abolition of the Georgian monarchy by the Russians, shortly after their arrival.

The Prince was the grandson of King Erekle II (who ruled 1762 - 1798), effectively the last King of Georgia (save the three insignificant years of King George XII until 1801 when Russia annexed Eastern Georgia). His mother was Princess Tekla and father, Vakhtang Jambakur-Orbeliani, who died during the suppression of one of the Kakheti rebellions in 1812. In his memoirs Alexandre tells of Vakhtang's great sorrow when bidding goodbye to his then pregnant wife Tekla, before heading off to battle. His was a life filled with tragedy and contradiction - torn between his duty to the Russian Emperor's direct instructions to fight against his own countrymen, and his instinctive love and commitment to his fellow Georgians.

Historians claim Vakhtang's death may not have been quite as his family told it - though don't specify how. But either way, Alexandre declared his father sought his own end deliberately - a story also backed up by his granddaughter Mariam. Certainly it can't be denied, his instructions from Russia to put down the rebellion would have left him in a state of inner conflict. Such a condition is a fate not uncommon to many Georgians down through history, due to its long string of invaders and numerous harsh conquests. In fact relatively speaking, the Russians were among the more benign.

Alexandre's romanticism was undoubtedly enriched by his royal blood, and the fact his mother, Princess Tekla, was the youngest and favourite child of King Erekle II.

Princess Tekla, was another strong personality. As a child she was known for dressing up as a boy. She wanted to be brought up and educated like her brothers - which she mostly was. Her father once even joked that she ought to be re-named 'Boy Tekla.' This explains her expertise in fencing and shooting – which is still seen in young Georgian women today. In her later years, when walking through the Sololaki hills in Tbilisi, young men, knowing her reputation, often handed her guns, then challenged her to shoot the nearest bird. According to reports, she never missed. But whether true or not, she always maintained a shrewd, politically-astute eye throughout her life. She ruled her three sons with the same tenacity, and none dared rebel - as she had.

However with the arrival of Alexandre's adulthood, this changed. The emotional door opened and out flew the instinct for rebellion.

Hence it was Alexandre who instigated the 1832 plot against Russian rule. He was caught and it failed. He then found himself exiled from Georgia for eight years – returning only in 1840, which many believe an extremely lenient punishment.

As mentioned, one price Russia imposed for providing military protection against the Persians, was abolition of the Georgian monarchy. As a consequence Alexandre's family lost most of its power, wealth, influence. But he maintained his sense of pride and quietly fought against the imposed changes, that effectively made Georgia a vassal state of the expanding Russian Empire.

After his eight years exile up north, he returned a different man. He avoided talking to strangers and at home, would give orders to blow out the candles after dinner, creating the impression everyone had gone to bed. Only then did he feel comfortable enough to talk freely with his guests.

But the failed rebellion gave him the kind of political experience and education he wouldn't have gained at home. He returned convinced Russian rule wouldn't help Georgia in any way; only strip out everything in the old country he held dear.

He blamed Russia for all unfavourable changes and skimmed over the many developments and benefits. But living his double-life, he'd still a number of close Russian friends; even chose one Toma Sherbashov, as his personal physician and confidant.

But in his eyes all the political changes were negative; purely the result of abolishing the noble line of Georgian kingship. The nation's history had been usurped by 'a fistful of rogues,' and the only way to right its wrongs was for Russia to leave. To encourage this process he made sure that he embodied personally all the noble qualities of the past and his illustrious grandfather's world.

Alexandre refused to accept the new era, and felt unhappy at the dropping of some little-used letters from the Georgian alphabet. Similarly he pointedly rejected all modern European styles of dress, with one notable exception - the wig.

CHAPTER 1

Facing the dilemma of all Orbeliani males, rapid hair loss, Alexandre quietly adopted this most popular of western vanities. He wore a wig just about all the time, to the extent that many of his closer friends remained completely ignorant of his concealed shiny dome.

But for this one peccadillo, he stayed true to his role as 'man of tradition.' He walked the capital sporting an old-fashioned coat, wide trousers and thin leather boots - the kind formerly worn by nobility - and in the proud gait due to his station.

His traditionalist attitude further revealed itself when Russia began discussing the abolition of serfdom – a controversial issue across both nations.

Alexandre didn't agree. He said that while the proposal might be well suited to the crueller and more unreasonable serfdom of Russia, in Georgia the relationship between serf and owner was more akin to that in an extended family. This is where Alexandre's romanticism possibly counted against him, for with the full self-centredness of a romantic, he believed others felt and believed just as him – including the treatment of serfs. Of course, not the case at all.

But true to his sense of benign nobility, he maintained the tradition of generosity right up to the end. He always gave away his three rouble, Royal pension to the Tbilisi poor - only of course, after he'd paid for his newspapers. But these he needed to glean news for everyone's benefits.

As for his claim of treating his serfs like an extended family. This was proved after his death when a huge crowd of mostly poor peasants, gathered around his house lamenting the loss of their generous prince. Certainly he was never a spendthrift and like most Georgian aristocracy, his income was always modest, in spite of possessing an estate.

As a way of extending his traditional way of life and influence, he took to publishing essays in the Georgian language magazine *Tsiskari*, ('Dawn') which he also supported financially. Here too he showed generosity. Once apparently, when the magazine looked likely to go under, three members of the editorial board arrived at his house, cap in hand. Alexandre is said to have promptly turned to his wife Katino Baratashvili, asking her to wheel out the silverware. In spite of her protestations, it was handed over, pawned and publication resumed.

'Can't let those scoundrels think we're so enslaved we can't save one little magazine', he declared.

CHARACTER in Georgia

As is common in Georgia, he maintained a jovial politeness even with people and nationalities he disliked - preferring comedy and nicknaming, to criticism. He invented the nickname *Rusinka* for his brother's famously beautiful wife - believing her secretly pro-Russian - in spite of his sibling's strong denials. A woman by the way, described by the French writer Alexander Dumas '*as the most physically striking and virtuous*' he'd ever met.

True to his love of comedy Alexandre even trained his dog to show its teeth and yelp to 'show us how you will smile when the Russians leave Georgia.' A clue perhaps to the roots of Georgia's highly praised theatrical tradition, noted for its caricature – honed during its long history of invasion. How over the centuries the need to criticise, of necessity, evolved into a more disarming and sophisticated style of comic impersonation.

Once he apparently said to his granddaughter, 'If I don't live long enough to see it, please come to my grave the day the Russians leave Georgia, and shout the news down at me.' Out of kindness Mariam Kobulashvili did apparently once go to the Sioni Cathedral and announce down to him, 'Rest in peace, they're gone!'

Even though they hadn't.

In summer Alexandre would travel to his country estate at Kazreti village where rumour had it, a former gold mine lay hidden. But apparently the Prince never heard this rumour. The family used to travel there in two springless wagons: one carrying him and extended family, the other, his numerous manuscripts, essential books and gifts.

The trip was long and required several rests and overnight stays, sweetened by bursts of Georgian traditional hospitality. Near the estate of his brother-in-law Zaal Baratashvili, the wagons had to be carried over a ravine due to no bridge – but done willingly by peasants in the nearby village. The Prince was known for his generosity and distribution of medicine and money.

But he was also known, later in life, for being similarly generous with his opinions. Again some romantic contradiction here. While he teased one sister-in-law for her love of Russia, his other sister-in-law, Katya Ilynskaya (wife of his brother Vakhtang), was half-Russian. And he greatly enjoyed her company, people saying they talked for hours.

CHAPTER 1

Although Alexandre never found out, he was secretly mocked for this. People said the only person he could find to oppose Russia was a Russian – and a woman, because no man would listen to him anymore.

Another romantic characteristic, applicable to both old and young generations, is the belief all humans are equal in the eyes of poetry. And Alexandre lived this out by loudly supporting the young Akaki Tsereteli, whose first poems were viciously criticized for using West-Georgian dialect. 'The best I've ever heard,' he declared to all who would listen.

Similarly he always treated his granddaughter Mariam as an equal. When she asked why he'd given her a nickname, he explained the new name was for a grown-up – which in his eyes, she was. She of course loved this. But still, even though he loved her no less, like a true nobleman, apparently only kissed her once.

The end of his days were spent in his mother's house in former Arkieli Square, near Sioni Cathedral, Tbilisi. Every evening he would step onto the balcony, look out toward his brothers' house and make the sign of the cross, before heading back inside to sleep.

They say once some thieves broke into the house, but on discovering it was Alexandre's, left empty-handed. Stealing from him, they said, would only leave him with less to give away.

Some say that in many ways, Alexandre was the last of his kind.

Chapter 2

The First Outlaw

Outlawism in Georgia – why is it so important?

First we should mention there's a subtle difference in attitude between the outlaw and robber. The outlaw breaks the law, but feels the laws are not written by the honest; that it requires the addition of some natural justice. While robbers just take for themselves. In Georgia the first tradition runs unusually deep. Some would say the outlaw wears a kind of romantic form of nobility. Others that the tradition has since been degraded – that the last true outlaws died out in the 1920s. This, in spite of that wild period in the early 1990s, just after the civil war, when for a couple of grim years the country seemed run by bandits - who believed they were noble. They had a name, *Mkhendrioni*, ('Horsemen' in English), and had an Anarchist leader.

But that's for another discussion – if not book.

Though speaking of literature – two important literary outlaws in Georgia do need to be called. The first, Koba, is the character created by the Georgian writer, Alexandre Kazbegi (1848-1893) in his most famous story *The Patricide*. Koba follows a kind of chivalric, Robin Hood-like life-style up in the Mokhevi-inhabited region of north Georgia (around Mt Kazbek). This story would become one of Joseph Stalin's favourites, and clearly a great influencer in his own character – for he chose the code-name Koba during his early Revolutionary years.

The other was one of Georgia's most popular novels from 1970s onwards. *Data Tutashkhia,* by Chabua Amirejibi, tells the adventures of a philosopher-outlaw, haunted by the fact that a genuine kind of justice or honesty hid inside all his criminality. Clearly linking in to Georgia's former outlaw/bandit tradition, the author has his character initiate a desperate kind of investigation through all the intricacies of love,

CHAPTER 2

religion, theft, friendship, betrayal, even murder, to a place beyond any political or social condemnation. Though one has to say, without any clear conclusion.

We might also mention Ilia Chavchavadze long poem *Pictures from a Robber's Life,* here too. A kind of manifesto against serfdom, born from the time when the boy Ilia accidentally encountered an outlaw walking in the woods.

But for us, the roots of that former, genuine outlaw, wend all the way back to the early 19th century Kartli, then the political heart of the country. For it is here they first made themselves known and then well-known, by their actions.

As for the reason they became so popular... Well, as we saw in the previous chapter, something had been going wrong with the Kartli aristocracy in the late 18th century. But a complex going-wrong, soon involving the country's newest overlords, the Russians. Change burst into the Georgian nation with the Russians' arrival, followed by the country's 1801 annexation. Some have argued, too rapidly and ill-led. But the full story is impossible to pin down. Certainly the worst of Georgia's aristocracy may have believed that with the weight of the Russian Emperor now behind them, they had carte-blanche for any kind of outrageous behaviour. For not only were they already the earth's natural-born royalty, now they'd been sanctioned as its legal administrators, thus by the same token, benefactors.

News of badly mistreated peasants gradually spread across the regions, and soon to the more politically savvy Kakhetians of Eastern Georgia. Why, they asked, did peasants allow themselves to be so wantonly subjugated? Could they not fight back? 'Your masters beat you and you simply run away to the forest,' they taunted.

At the same time, the reader might note, wasn't our own Alexandre Jambakur-Orbeliani also one of those Princes from Kartli? The answer is yes, but living towards the less-bad end of the noble spectrum, where a number of non-malicious aristocrats still holed out. But the fact can't be avoided – he too sold his serfs, as revealed by Zakaria Chichinadze (1853-1931), the scholar and expert of that period.

But there were other, worse tales. Like serfs being flogged like animals by their so-called noble masters, being sold-on like cattle, or swapped for hunting dogs. Way too many were forced to work in truly inhuman conditions and for excessive hours. But most notorious of all were the cases of 'first night rights,' a crime then still tacitly permitted to the aristocracy. This resulted in a number of illegitimate children born of peasant girls.

Zakaria Chichinadze recounts how one old Prince boasted loudly of his tally – 'I had well over thirty girls just called Mariam.'

As that drip, drip, drip of shameful behaviour gradually mounted, the stories spread like a stain into the popular mind.

Around then came the story of a peasant in Kakheti, eastern Georgia, who, while minding his pigs, was suddenly confronted by a well-dressed and armed stranger. The stranger demanded one pig as a present. The peasant politely refused, so the stranger simply shot a pig, then instructed the owner to carry it down to the place where he and his companions prepared a meal. When the indignant peasant refused again, the stranger merely punched him, grabbed him by the legs, trussed the pig over his shoulders, then dragged them both down the hill to the waiting feast or '*supra*' table (a Georgian feast).

His already well-lubricated companions watched this display approvingly, insisting the peasant roast his own pig on the spit. When cooked to their satisfaction, the men invited the pig owner, now recovered, to join their feast. When all was finished, in a magnanimous gesture, the peasant was provided with financial compensation and told emphatically, not to 'refuse hospitality' next time.

This was followed by another armed *supra*-intervention, also in Kakheti. Three brothers, having finished working in their vineyard, were also confronted by a similar, no less muscular, pistol-wearing stranger. He insisted on joining their meal, though perhaps less stridently than previously. With his invitation duly accepted the meal proceeded. And it wasn't long before, in true Georgian *supra*-style, the stranger became just another member of the laughing, joking, drinking company. All part of that great equalizing process of every good Georgian table - facilitated of course by Kakhetian wine. At the end of the meal the stranger suddenly introduced himself. 'I am Arsena,' he said, explaining that although from Kartli, he was currently having to spend some time away from home - in Kakheti.

The brothers knew exactly who he was of course, and why he was avoiding home. Here was the legendary Arsena Odzelashvili (1797–

CHAPTER 2

1842), Georgia's most well-known outlaw, renowned for appearing suddenly out of the forest, unashamedly appropriating whatever he wished, then disappearing. But often unexpectedly repaying it and with interest. Some indeed say that in the first half of the 19th century Arsena became the most famous man in Georgia. And judging from the number of surviving poems, stories and legends linked to his name, this may be true.

Which makes his presence in Georgian culture particularly important. Some say a significant part of the bedrock underlying the national character.

For in fact Arsena was only one of a growing fraternity of outlaws in Kartli, due to the region's unusually harsh treatment of peasants. Because Arsena tended to rob the rich and distribute his spoils among the poor, locals came to respect him and protect his identity.

Indeed it is said that when Arsena was in residence at his Ikalto village hideout, near Telavi (in Kakheti, eastern Georgia), the local peasants felt safer because the north Caucasian Lezgins held back their customary raids into Georgia, fearing the legend of this bandit.

As time went on, Arsena's reputation grew, and he started to make ever bolder appearances across this and other regions. In fact so frequently it became slightly strange, until it was discovered that other bandits were borrowing his name. This to the degree that Arsena could be staging dramatic robberies in two wholly different places at the same time.

But his fame also proved another bonus, for those duty-bound to arrest him. Since photography, fingerprinting, DNA testing had yet to be invented, the authorities were happy to blame 'Arsena' for just about all their unsolved crimes – further polishing his reputation. This convenient fact was much aided by his skilled self-concealment in Georgia's extensive forests. Thanks to the dense tree-cover, just like Robin Hood in England's Sherwood Forest, he remained at large for unusually long, for such a well-known criminal.

However there is a difference between Arsena and Robin Hood – Arsena actually existed, whereas no one person has ever been proved, the real Robin.

As for the truth behind the Georgian legend; it is widely believed that Arsena was only a nickname – his real name was Ioseb (Joseph). His family, all peasants, hailed from the village of Marabda, fifty kilometres south of Tbilisi, where his father worked for Prince Baratashvili, in fact none other than our Alexandre Jambakur-Orbeliani's brother-in-law, Zaal. It is also said that the young Arsena was then sent to another village, where he was raised and baptised by his new godfather's family.

But the legendary qualities of Arsena's life and exploits kept increasing, with a life of their own. One in particular was his reputation as a lover. Handsome from childhood, tall, with narrow waist and broad shoulders, rumour had it he could chase a run-away cart downhill, catch and stop it with ease. Also, that he possessed a famously generous nature; bountiful in its charm and opinions. This, some claim, is what launched Arsena into banditry in the first place - a case of frustrated love.

Folk poems tell the story of a man falling in love with his master's maid, at a time when local custom decreed a serf could never marry a member of the landlord's household. So Arsena eloped with her to Kartli, the region he knew best. They hid out at his secret base under the limestone cliffs at Birtvisi Canyon, while he tried to find a priest to legitimize their love in marriage.

But because his wife-to-be was not formally released by her owner, every priest refused – forcing Arsena into an unwilling life of sin in the Birtvisi caves. But the couple survived, even flourished there due to Arsena's great friendship with the foresters, who brought them all the food and drink they needed – no doubt in exchange for some banditry spoils.

But facing a future of bringing up a family in concealment for the rest of their lives, Arsena eventually plumbed for the most practical solution. Reluctantly he returned his no-longer bride-to-be back to her master, Prince Baratashvili. At which point his banditry began in earnest.

There is a well-known *Arsena's Poem,* passed down orally, usually in song and by Racha bagpipers. Although constantly embellished, it was finally printed, by one Petre Umikashvili. The poem would soon become epic, finding itself republished into at least 70 separate editions over the ensuing decades. A significant number for that time. Indeed some claim it the most popular Georgian poem of the era.

Naturally the text romanticised Arsena's ardour, claiming he loved his bride-to-be so passionately, he gallantly sacrificed his former peaceful life for one of noble banditry, purely for her sake. But other sources claim Arsena in fact had three wives. That the first, as stated, he returned to his master. The second he abducted, or bride-snatched, although also out of love, but unfortunately she died. The third he then lived with secretly in Tbilisi, remarrying after the death of his second wife.

There is another equally plausible theory that his first and the second wives were in fact the same person, twice abducted; that the total of wives had been multiplied by the oral tradition. However one fact cannot be refuted. In spite of all the heroism and romance, daily life for any outlaw is ultimately hard.

Years of constant robbery, hiding one's self and booty; the endlessly changing identity, constrict life options considerably, especially for a couple. Eventually, if wanting a family, they'd best begin their lives again in some remote place, away from gossip, probably in the service of a new master. In Georgia at that time, such a place tended to be the Muslim area around Akhaltsikhe – then not part of the Russian Empire.

Thus, it was eventually here that a fugitive-weary Arsena and his 'wife' settled with the family of Padre Shahkuliani, who incidentally was a Catholic, and tolerated as such.

Soon however they encountered a problem. Somehow it was discovered that Arsena and his wife never in fact married. Thus their hosts were convention-bound to return the couple to fugitive status – which neither party wanted.

Fortunately circumstances came to the rescue – no doubt aided by some Robin Hood generosity. A marriage ceremony was hastily arranged in the city's Catholic church. Legend has it that Arsena expressed his gratitude by providing sufficient gallons of wine and enough Kartli sheep to invite the whole of Christian Akhaltsikhe to his wedding feast.

Thus our hero was able to live on as an immigrant down in Akhaltsikhe, along with many other refugee peasants from Kartli. Records show he wasn't the only one escaping the cruelty of its landlords or their unjust rules and conventions. Seemed even those of former outlaw status could live out a relatively peaceful life, just below the southern border of the then Russian Empire.

This might be a good time to note that banditry wasn't the only means of getting even with Georgia's iniquitous feudalism. While a select few like Arsena opted for the extreme life of an outlaw or highwayman, others simply employed a more direct method – such as hiring men like 'Zose the Ossetian.'

Statue to Arsena at the entrance to Mtshketa

CHAPTER 2

Some groups of peasants set up private funds to pay such pseudonymed strangers to eliminate their problems permanently – by assassination. But here too lay another potential injustice. Years of accumulated bitterness could result in a savagery worse than that inflicted on the indentured victims. On one occasion a group of peasants massacred the entire family of Prince Sumbatashvili, down to the tiniest infant.

As for Arsena, it is said he never killed anyone during his acts of robbery. A bandit very much from the no-blood school. Folk tradition also tells of his many sophisticated, even charming methods of robbery – no doubt slightly romanticised. That afterwards he would try to redistribute as much as he had taken. Although with one notable exception – livestock – whose determined and steady accumulation seemed to be Arsena's trademark.

Some historians claim that after a while Arsena didn't need to keep robbing. That in the outlaw hierarchy he remained relatively well-off. For although living in Akhaltsikhe, he frequently travelled to Kartli to survey his growing flock of sheep – entrusted to a reliable friend. Thus he appeared to have a semi-legit and steady source of income. Some claim he possessed several flocks and in various locations – following a kind of middle-class outlaw lifestyle down in Akhaltsikhe. History has shown that many successful outlaws normally retire at this point. But not Arsena, for he had a cause beyond his own; as a kind of voice of the people.

Then came the inevitable day when the Russian army moved south and added the Akhaltsikhe region to their Empire - along with the rest of the Caucasus. But interestingly, Arsena decided not to keep running by retreating deeper into the Ottoman Empire. Rather he changed his modus-operandi, returning to Kartli to become more of an on-the-road style highwayman. And in so doing, even more of a household name in Eastern Georgia.

Soon he became so popular with the peasants, nearly every other boy born to a serf family came to be named Arsena or claimed to have been one of Arsena's many godchildren. For it seems that Arsena was a committedly religious man, and the Georgian Orthodox Church allows up to four godfathers to each child (in practice sometimes even more). The great majority of peasants seemed to enjoy the association with such

24

a brave, freedom-loving criminal. Thus more and more of the country became Arsena's kingdom, like a kind of inverse, criminal nobility.

So what was it in Arsena's law-breaking that made him so popular? Ironically it may have more to do with fairness and justice. As if his thieving served as more than mere retribution, or extracting a tribute from the rich, but the enforcement of a kind of natural, people's law, bypassing the injustices of feudalism. That this bandit's lifestyle emanated from a place closer to genuine fairness than any the state could offer.

For instance, for many years after Arsena's death, if two men were arguing in Kartli, both utterly convinced they were right, one would almost certainly demand that 'you measure your argument with Arsena's yardstick.'

Although the phase isn't used in modern Georgia, it stems from another Arsena story. This describes him walking through local markets checking the fabric benchmarks used by local merchants, to see if they'd been shortened from the standard.

During his later and riskier highwayman phase, Arsena became more visible, roving extensively among Georgia's growing network of roads. This was the time when Russian-style inns started to appear, allowing travellers to overnight, refresh their horses, then resume their journey next morning.

He became a regular in such inns. But not too regular. Due to the requirements of his trade, he never lingered for long. But it's incorrect to say his main residence was the forest. At that time, indeed even in earlier periods, he could usually find a friendly bed for the night in just about any village. However if soldiers were reported coming that way, Arsena wouldn't be there. On this point he remained fastidious – which probably helped maintain his exceptionally long life as a bandit.

But he had one weakness - his instinctive sociability. He found it hard to resist a good local inn, offering its wide selection of human company. Also a place he'd be further able to indulge his cause of natural justice.

These countryside traveller's inns soon became popular meeting points for all walks of life. Customers would gather together, sit cheek-by-jowl in the dining areas. Indeed some claim these guest houses as the nation's most democratic establishments – purely from necessity.

CHAPTER 2

Normally their interior contained a single main room furnished with one long table. The simplicity of design forced princes, priests, peasants and officers to eat elbow to elbow – unimaginable anywhere else.

And it was fairly unlikely anyone would recognise Arsena in these inns. This was a time more of verbal, than facial recognition. By maintaining a watchful eye, this famous outlaw could still enjoy conversations with strangers, catch up on latest gossip, voice opinions and of course, gather vital news snippets for future robberies.

Lest one become too enamoured with thievery, it should also be noted that Arsena, especially in his later years, was not always the walking embodiment of natural justice, as some poems indicate. Sources report that once sufficiently drunk and in certain company, Arsena was only too happy to provoke a fight. But due to his peasant origins he preferred to swing more at outsiders, officers or nobility, rather than fellow serfs. However, as we shall see later, not always the case.

As he grew older, these occasions became more frequent. While some say Arsena never murdered anyone during a robbery, he did once kill a man. This event apparently happened at the inn frequented by the nobleman Saginashvili. The story goes that they were sitting and drinking happily enough together, until a fairly drunk Arsena let loose a way-too-honest opinion about the Russian Emperor.

'Son of a dog!'

Saginashvili immediately protested, demanding that he take it back, as his, '…life's allegiance is sworn to that man.'

An increasingly violent argument ensued, finally requiring the intervention of several customers. Legend has it that Saginashvili promptly stood up to leave the room, at which point Arsena, fearing he headed straight to the local police station, shot him in the back. In fact the nobleman merely headed for the outdoors toilet. As he died Saginashvili turned to Arsena,

'What have you done… I was only going to pee.'

Anyway that's what they say.

Whichever the case, the fact of this death was certainly due to some kind of misunderstanding. And if Arsena was the culprit, he never repeated such an act.

But as with many of the Arsena stories, reasons for doubt hang in the air. Firstly, Arsena was raised in the Saginashvili estate, so he may have been linked to the family as a godchild (Princes would often take on that role for their peasants in Georgia). This would make a deliberate murder far less likely. Secondly, the crime could well have been committed by one of the 'false' Arsenas. Thirdly, *Arsena's Poem* never even hinted at such an episode – though of course romanticisation may be to blame here.

Another practical reason for Arsena's presence in these inns, is the information they supplied on new targets.

A particular favourite came in the form of visiting nobility from Western Georgia, on hunting-dog selling missions. These Imeretian aristocrats would parade their famously trained animals across the country - particularly to Kartli and Kakheti – engaging in the notorious practice of dog-exchange for serfs. As a serf himself, this practice deeply offended Arsena. So he and his fellows devised a few disruptions to the trade.

This soon turned into a kind of business - though more the specialty of other outlaws, like one called Porakishvili. His technique would be to emerge from the forest bristling with weapons, just as the Imeretian noblemen were leaving Kartli – demanding payment for their continued safe passage out of East Georgia. This amounted to their full contingent of newly gained serfs – who would immediately be released. Invariably the dog breeders handed them over – to then receive the threat of far more drastic treatment should they try to again ply their trade in East Georgia.

Might this be a form of natural justice? Well, at least a beyond-the-law means of providing something that today would be very much within-the-law.

But Arsena's methods were slightly more ingenious than Porakishvili's. He preferred to sidle up to the nobleman in the inn, get him well drunk, steal his key, then creep up the stairs and free the young serfs locked in the room.

Because this became an ever more common practice, Arsena soon found himself actively hunted by the noblemen's military friends. This required an ever-wider variety of overnight venues. Fortunately, due to his former life, they remained plentiful – though he still needed to maintain high-level caution.

It is said he was once betrayed by someone called Parsadan from the village of Bodbiskhevi, then arrested. But not too long after, he

CHAPTER 2

escaped while taking a prisoner's bath in Tbilisi's Abanoturbani district. Although Arsena was chained to the wall, his friends had befriended the guards with enough rum-laced wine that soon the soldiers could hardly recognise each other, let alone their prisoner. With a supplied file, Arsena doggedly cut through the chain, then disappeared back into his forests.

He also applied the same caution to priests. Arsena was a religious man and regularly took communion in the village of Koda. He could sometimes be spotted as the only person not dismounted from his horse. He always kept one foot remaining in the stirrup, ready for an emergency gallop to freedom.

But ultimately it wasn't the police, but Arsena's hot-headedness, especially when drunk, that brought about his end. At first this only landed him in embarrassing situations, but they developed.

Friedrich von Bodenstedt, a German traveller and poet, recalls one such incident. At a religious celebration in the mountains, a tall, well-dressed man was pointed out to him as the outlaw Arsena. He describes an impressive figure, slightly less lavishly dressed than a noble, but who without any provocation, began an argument with an officer, then demanded his sword. The row escalated to the extent that women were finally called-in to break it up. It worked, but only after the officer surrendered his sword.

The next day, realising he'd misjudged the officer, Arsena returned the sword together with a second one, as an apology.

On another evening his friend, the priest Iakob Barnov, while leading a bridal party between mountain villages, was met by a group of agitated locals bearing torches. They warned that a, 'in one of his moods,' Arsena waited round the corner, threatening to kidnap the bride.

Iakob promised to talk to Arsena, and spurred his horse. But Arsena seeing the horse not the man, fired his pistol - fortunately missing. Iakob then shouted at Arsena, who recognizing his friend, apologised profusely. The next day he sent Iakob a new horse, a gun and some presents for the bride.

In the later stages of his life Arsena is believed to have returned to live in Tbilisi, secretly. After the death of his second wife, he re-married and rented a small, flat-roofed house in Kldis Urbani, ('rock quarter') immediately under the Narikala Fortress. Although the entire neighbourhood knew the young woman as an outlaw's wife, nobody betrayed either of them. Thus he maintained a secret life right to the end, returning home only at night. Some say he even owned a small inn close to an entrance of the city, often serving behind the counter.

Whether these stories are true or not, Arsena continued his criminal life right up to his death, dividing time between Kartli and Kakheti. And he seemed to maintain his cause of people's justice – believing strongly in the abolition of serfdom. But this wouldn't happen until 1864 in Georgia, long after his death.

With the subsequent publication of *Arsena's Poem*, the developing Arsena stories and myths would provide superb material for many writers and poets. Among the most famous were Ilia Chavchavadze and Akaki Tsereteli, the latter writing a play about him – which helped the Arsena story live on into the Soviet period. The Communists then held him up as a noble warrior for the proletariat – even if by then nearly all truth had been thoroughly blended with imagination. In 1933 the acclaimed writer Mikheil Javakhishvili (1880-1937) wrote his longest novel *Arsena of Marabda*. But it was with a deeply ironic twist that Javakhishvili would shortly end up shot in the terrible 1937 purges, having been officially declared an 'enemy of the people' – not unsimilar to Arsena. There was also the eponymous film *Arsena,* by Mikheil Chiaureli (1937) and, in Soviet times, a monument in Mtskheta by the river. This stone statue by E. Machabeli (1947), was later replaced by a bronze copy in 1997. It remains there to this day.

As for the moment of Arsena's death – this happened at Mtskheta, Georgia's ancient capital. And as with most of history's epic characters, his end carried a full dose of pathos.

That day Arsena sat by the roadside, possibly at his own inn, before a simple picnic of wine, bread, cheese and curds, ready for anyone who cared to join. By then, when the wine flowed too liberally, so did Arsena's hot-headedness. And it was this that summoned his nemesis.

It came in the form of a militiaman called Giorgi Sepiskveradze, from the village of Ubisa. Another strikingly strong man, famed for fighting the Lezgins – North Caucasian raiders who liked to attack the Kakhetian peasants. Although also a peasant, but from Imereti, he owned a parcel of land in the village of Kuchatani, hence his nickname, Kuchatneli.

CHAPTER 2

The two met on the road near Mtskheta beside Arsena's spread of food. The poems recount it was a Good Friday, the one day in Lent when Orthodox believers should refrain from alcohol.

But Arsena was drinking, so maybe it wasn't Good Friday. Either way Giorgi Sepiskveradze was heading west to his native Imereti for Easter. The poem also mentions a young man accompanied him – as his Lezgin batman.

There are two versions of this story. But in both, Kuchatneli and his companion arrive at Arsena's picnic to be offered wine, but they refused – possibly due to it being Good Friday. They continued their journey, but for some reason this infuriated the outlaw, who chased them down on horseback. An argument ensued and Arsena hit Giorgi with the flat of his sword. The reply came back as a flashing blade, cutting deep into Arsena's arm. Arsena reached for the dagger in his boot, but the Lezgin immediately shot him dead in the back.

The second version tells of a vicious fight between the two older men, as Giorgi's 'nephew' watches on, then is struck brutally by Arsena – at which point Giorgi shoots Arsena dead.

In the folk poem Arsena had a prophetic dream. In it he paints his own beard with blood – which could help explain the undertone to the event.

But whatever really happened, Arsena died where he spent most of his life – on the road. And maybe it wasn't a wholly unjustified death. But neither was it dishonourable, or his name wouldn't have lasted, to become transformed into the Georgian Everyman – embodying the thoughts, problems, pain of his fellow peasants.

As Arsena lay on the road, Kuchatneli still had no idea who he'd killed. After discovering his true identity, he refused the reward money. Indeed the poem includes a scene with him trying to reason against the fight with Arsena, saying there could be no point in it for either of them.

So why did those two honourable men meet and the famous outlaw die?

They say the endless, fugitive life of an outlaw hardens the soul. That heroes often fall victim to their own former strengths, unable to bend with the times. In Arsena's day the criminal life usually lasted two, perhaps three years. Those making it to eight or ten were considered legendary. Arsena exceeded them all. And even when he died, his life continued to live on in others - still claiming to be him.

Arsena's body is believed to be buried somewhere in Mtskheta. Fifty years after his death Davit Kezeli, a journalist, commissioned a gravestone with the inscription: 'Here lies the great outlaw Arsena Odzelashvili'. And 'Arsena's Poem' ends with the words: 'He was a good man of this world, so let the light shine on him in the next.'

Certainly the love of this man's legend remains strong in Georgia. What did disappear of Arsena was his money. The poem states he'd stashed a good portion of his life's achievement somewhere secure. But to this day it's not been found.

But is that relevant?

In a way it is. Because Arsena's life coincided with the period in Georgian history when rebellion had become fashionable. It could even be said that Alexandre Jambakur-Orbeliani merely acted as another kind of rebel, an aristocratic one, fighting the cruelty and injustice of Russian rule. Like Arsena's, this noble rebellion also failed. Emperor Nicholas I would later arrive in Tbilisi to witness a parade through the city to Madatov's Island (by today's Dry Bridge), celebrating his new Georgian addition to the Empire - while numerous Georgians were still being sent away into exile.

As for Arsena's buried treasure... maybe it had been of a different kind. Not physical money or gold – which disappeared anyway. More that longer lasting, emotional currency. The type that glitters in the eyes of all human beings following noble causes.

It could even be said, his treasure - which he wished to the poor - still remains in the Georgian soil, buried somewhere not far from the old town of Kaspi, near Mtskheta, in the very heart of Kartli. That it will probably always remain there, ready for discovery in the popular mind, again and again.

Chapter 3

Birth of the Poet – Nikoloz Baratashvili

Europeanism entered Georgia in its many and various ways. The country's more oriental culture of the pre-Russian centuries would soon receive a political and cultural hammering from the north, after entering the Russian Empire.

Thus it might be said the new Europe-orientated era started one autumn day in the mid 1830s near Tbilisi, in the thoughts and feelings of one young Georgian aristocrat – and voracious Russian language reader.

Nikoloz Baratashvili (1817–1845), later hailed as the Georgian Byron, had just been challenged to a duel by his uncle, the military officer and future memoir author, Ilia Orbeliani (1818-1853). Although the description 'nephew' hardly fit, for his uncle was barely two years older, more akin to a brother.

Nikoloz, until then known far more for his pranks than poetry, and egged-on by an even more impudent friend Magalashvili, could never resist poking fun at the 'young and courageous' officer Ilia. In public if at all possible.

But the relentless, even obsessive prankery carried a more poetic undertone, expressing some of the restless, provocative modernity pouring down into the Caucasus from the salons and publishing houses of Europe. A powerful literary imagery that would soon reach into every level of society – and whose effects still linger on today.

The circumstances behind the duel began at a party of mutual friends. Orbeliani had been dreading the event, fearing more ostentatious mockery from his nephew, which he felt he never deserved. So much so he decided that if it continued, this time he'd end it with the method he knew best – pistols. Duelling in those days was still a popular pastime, usually involving military officers, but also the occasional enfant terrible. Indeed Russia's arguably two greatest poets Alexander Pushkin (1799-1837) and Mikhail Lermontov (1814-1841), both died in duels around that time - Lermontov actually in the north Caucasus, during one of his army postings.

So the air was already well charged with the new and growing romance of self-immolation.

As fate would have it, while Nikoloz arrived at the party as planned, his provocateur friend Magalashvili never showed. But this didn't dampen Nikoloz's lust for satire. And with Ilia already so pre-wound, it didn't take long for him to switch the duelling demand to his nephew – who immediately accepted.

A time and place was arranged, seconds appointed – Magalashvili for Nikoloz and a fellow officer for Ilia. When the hour came, the duellers were accompanied by the usual group of eager spectators. Most, it has to be said, supporting the underdog Nikoloz, in his gallant defiance of the military-trained Ilia.

But the outcome seemed foregone – in favour of the soldier. The place chosen for the duel was an escarpment on the outskirts of the city with a view of the high Caucasus - where the tall, athletic Ilia soon stood looking down on the shorter Nikoloz below.

The seconds checked the pistols and handed them to the duellists. The first shot was fired by Nikoloz – who missed his uncle. Ilia then aimed and pulled his trigger. But the pistol simply spluttered and nothing happened. Suspecting foul play, an even more enraged Ilia grabbed his second pistol, aimed, then fired again.

This time Nikoloz cried and fell to the ground clutching his chest. At which point Ilia, suddenly horrified at what he'd just done – killing his own flesh and blood, and now facing the task of breaking the news to his family – rushed over. Leaning down to check Nikoloz's wound, he suddenly heard his nephew whisper, 'Hey, stop stealing raisins from my pocket!'

Everyone burst out laughing, already guessing Nikoloz's sabotage of Ilia's gunpowder. Everyone that is, save Ilia himself who, although re-infuriated, soon found the anger overwhelmed by relief at not having slain his own nephew.

In the end the whole event resolved itself Georgian style, via a grand *supra* involving all parties – ensuring this family drama would be long celebrated.

CHAPTER 3

But inside this tale lay a deeper layer of meaning. One underlying Nikoloz's restless need to prank and eagerness to accept the duel. A kind of tragic heroism, or Byronism, then being inculcated into the Caucasus mostly by Russian army officers, many of them aspiring poets themselves. And it was this sentiment that would soon become fashionable throughout Georgian society, as it was in Western Europe, with lasting cultural influence – as still evident in the ongoing spiritualisation of nature.

For underneath Baratashvili's practical jokes and impudent, youthful demeanour, lay a profound philosophical despair at the human condition – of the kind finding voice in Lermontov's poem *The Demon*, or Lord Byron's *The Corsair*, (*'the man of loneliness and mystery'*). A feeling that would merit a far wider exploration than his short life and only 37 poems would allow – even though today, he is often regarded as Georgia's finest poet.

During his life only a relatively small circle of Tbilisi society even knew of his poetry, which circulated mostly among friends and family. So what was the reason for this prankster's version of Romantic despair?

Let's take a look at this section of his poem,

Thoughts on the Mtkvari River Bank

So deep in melancholy
I headed to the river bank
to swim sad thoughts
through the water.
I found my familiar place
tears misting soft grass.
The world was wrong
in the water floated a piece of clear sky...

Why is my life wasted
I don't know.
Why is our life
a vessel never filled...

CHARACTER in Georgia

Nikoloz Baratashvili - 'Tato' - by the painter Lado Gudiashvili

Certainly human culture was the culprit - along with the European Romantics who had sewn seductive glimpses of that they called the Sublime - a kind of invisible natural order that to them, every soul had a duty to pursue.

But before looking too loftily that direction, it might be useful to first glance at the emotional priming provided by the poet's Tbilisi childhood and upbringing.

Nikoloz Baratashvili was born out of a marriage between two grand aristocratic families. His mother, Epemia, hailed from the Orbeliani clan, sister of three celebrated army officers – Grigol, Zakaria and Ilia. His father, Meliton, came from the wealthy and influential Baratashvilis, but managed to squander most of his inheritance on lavish hospitality and feasts. His natural generosity had turned to profligacy and soon accumulated significant debts. This personality defect cut a deep vein of disenchantment into his son.

CHAPTER 3

Due to Meliton's love of hospitality, many Georgian nobles and high-ranking Russians became regular visitors to the Baratashvili home – providing Nikoloz with a cornucopia of high-flowing conversation during his childhood. Meliton's was the nobility of the past, as discussed in Chapter 1 – intrinsically rather than intelligently noble – and thus showing little concern for the future.

When alone with his family Meliton's insecurity rose to the surface in terrible rages – tantrums so loud, the whole neighbourhood could hear. These became more prominent when the household downsized to a new home near Mukhrani Bridge (today's 17 Chakrukhadze St - now the Baratashvili Museum).

On the plus side, Meliton Baratashvili also spoke a number of languages, which the Russian authorities found extremely helpful, and paid him for his services. Good translators of the many Caucasian languages were few. This explains why Meliton remained in favour, in spite of his temper and regular fist fights with Chancellor's office officials.

But the same irascibility also turned against his son. Nikoloz would too often be on the receiving end of unwarranted physical attacks – further scarring his personality.

The couple would have fourteen children, but most died in infancy. Only Nikoloz and his three sisters made it to adulthood. As the family's sole male heir, he found himself pampered by his mother and nicknamed Tato. Probably his mother's intense devotion gave Tato the confidence to develop his impudence and imagination.

It might also be noted, Nikoloz wasn't just a writer. From an early age he impressed all with his dancing, particularly the local Georgian style. The Caucasus has a strong, indigenous dance tradition - then mostly folk, as with the popular 'Lezginka;' and the various Sufi dances, such as the 'zikr'. And dance is the place where strong emotion finds confident placement into the body. Noticed at school, he received a personal instructor who then taught him modern European dance – which he later put to flamboyant use in parties and balls.

But Tbilisi of the 1830s was only a small provincial capital of some 25,000, with no theatre, or even newspapers. The main entertainment for those like Tato had become strolling in the parks, going to balls or making endless social visits – like to Manana Orbeliani's salon, where participants would spend hours in earnest, unedifying gossip. The city seemed almost to require the exploits of Baratashvili and his misbehaving friends, without which it would surely have been little better than a deadish, garrison town.

Added to this came the eternal threat of plague, which Tato never feared and liked to use as a metaphor – once complaining to his officer uncle in a letter, *'Tbilisi is a place full of babble and the bubonic.'* But as a compulsive reader, his prankery started to connect with its verbal cousin, poetry. Soon he was indulging the attitudes of other bourgeoisie-critical Romantics, who aimed their souls towards Revolution and the Sublime. A feeling hinted at in his poem about the nearby ***Aragvi*** river

> *Aragvi, Aragviani,*
> *your mountains*
> *follow you shouting.*
> *Your shore is tireless with waves*
> *calm rests on your banks.*
> *How could anyone not stop*
> *look at you?*
> *How could any Georgian*
> *not dismount his heart*
> *on your banks.*
> *When he sees your beauty*
> *he can't sleep*
> *even sip his wine*
> *rest the horse to eat your grass...*
> *He must wet his forehead with your water*
> *shout one time*
> *Aragvi...!*
> *at your green mountains.*
> *Then he'll never care about being late.*
> *As the setting sun spreads*
> *its giant pleasure*
> *over the old tent*
> *that looks out*
> *at a river*
> *so full to bursting*

(A free translation by the authors)

CHAPTER 3

The Romantic ideas encountered in his European reading encouraged his misbehaviour, then reputation as a notorious flirt. Here he showed what could be called, a Byronic disregard for ladies' ages, social or marital standings. But in spite of his romantic successes, none evolved into anything serious – even though he declared his great request from life was for a soul-mate. Once he even wrote despairingly to an uncle that Tbilisi could offer his roaming, restless heart nothing – even though he still loved the city dearly. A feeling slightly different from other Romantics who, like Lermontov, declared '*my soul has been corrupted by my society... all that's left for me is travel*' (in *Hero of Our Time.*) Baratashvili still seemed loyal to his home city and country.

This profound, spiritual dissatisfaction, echoed perhaps by Byron's phrase, '*I who deny nothing, but doubt everything,*' remained central to his personality, and the growing Romantic movement across Europe.

One of his biographers tried to explain it by the fact that Nikoloz had been blocked both from experiencing university, and its alternative – travel. Another, that he failed to make a name for himself in the Caucasian wars, as other poets (like Lermontov) did, or his friend Levan Melikishvili (1817-1892) – who eventually achieved the rank of general. But as a child Nikoloz had broken both legs when falling downstairs, to find one healing slightly shorter than the other – causing a limp, inspiring comparisons with Byron's club foot.

On leaving school he asked his father to arrange a military career, only to be told bluntly, 'go and join the disabled regiment.' Tato's next request, to attend university, was met by a similar rude refusal from his spendthrift father, who then declared himself about to die.

'And when I'm gone you'll be needed by the family!'

In fact Meliton recovered quickly, outliving his son by fifteen years. But with all his ambitions squashed, Tato accepted the role as clerk in a law firm. Not really the profession for Georgia's foremost Romantic poet - though nobody knew it then. But once in the office he couldn't restrain the pranking impulse - inventing absurd rumours, just to see how much would be believed by his gullible colleagues.

After work each day he'd then set out on 'missions,' roving house to house, making uninvited visits under the guise of delivering news and gossip. And the doors nearly always opened – save a few in the more conservative porches, or when his gossip fantasies went too far, leaving him standing rejected and disbelieved on doorsteps.

At work he proved himself well and indeed so efficient, his superiors predicted a long and esteemed office career. But his dreams lay a world away, aiming at military glory with all its possibilities of Tbilisi escape, grand emotional adventures, and poetry of the Sublime.

For a while it seemed literature would be his only means of travel, along perhaps with the emotional journeys afforded by a few love excursions. And some would produce powerful lyrical poems. His friend Levan Melikishvili (later to become assistant Viceroy to the Caucasus) tells of the day he met an agitated Tato, who'd just encountered the beautiful Ekaterine Chavchavadze. Apparently Tato sat down and there and then wrote one of his finest poems – *Earring*. It opens,

> *A butterfly,*
> *slowly rippling,*
> *on a spotless lily...*

He claimed the sunlight glinting on the jewel, drove him to a frenzy that had to be written out - to save himself. Biographers note that Nikoloz wasn't particularly handsome, especially when set against Tbilisi's many impressive military officers – meaning he had to rely on personality rather than medals, to draw attention. And although he dressed with some flair and style, his lameness and short stature made him no match for the dashing, 'courageous' officers – like his uncle Ilia, with whom by the way, he'd made up.

Initially his only route to significance seemed professional. But even here he lacked appropriate education and qualifications for the civil service's higher ranks.

However the swell of urban life in Tbilisi, Russia's ongoing Caucasian war, its soldiers, stories and weaponry clanking around the streets - provided him with a brooding poetic background. The young Tato felt it intensely – especially when his uncle Ilia was taken prisoner by the Imam Shamil (1797-1871), the Empire's arch enemy. As was customary in the Caucasian wars, Ilia was thrown in a deep hole then held for ransom or exchange.

CHAPTER 3

Miraculously he survived. And one could almost say, ironically (given their history) Tato's most famous poem, *Merani* ('horse' or 'charger') is dedicated to him, or rather his ability to survive – like the black horse he vividly describes galloping across the Caucasian landscape:

It races, it flies, bears me on its back
follows no road, knows no path...
as the raven croaks just behind
with death-tinted eyes...

Perhaps the lack of military adventure pressurised Tato's poetry – as a substitute for the real thing. Who knows.

Looking through the correspondence with his uncles – who he used as information sources – one notices a huge variation in tone. For instance, he employs a deeper, more respectful voice for the older Grigol – as if addressing the father he never had.

By then Grigol Orbeliani already had the reputation of a celebrated military figure, having seen much action across the Caucasus. This included a number of battles against Shamil – who he'd later see captured and displayed at the court of Alexander II in St Petersburg. In letters home from Russia he described his Muslim foe as a noble, impressive man. That he regretted not having shown him due respect during his younger days – when so many other Russian officers declared Shamil 'our brave and great opponent', even 'dignified adversary'. The kind of words leading to Leo Tolstoy's novel *Hadji Murat*, describing another Avar tribal leader and former foe, set in the north Caucasus.

But being King Erekle II's great-grandson, the young Grigol would never have referred to one of Georgia's traditional enemies in such words. This had to wait until the wisdom of age (and victory). Like Tato, Grigol also carried ambitions as a poet, though he wrote in a more staid, early Romantic style – lacking Tato's original, revolutionary language.

It also might be said that Nikoloz and Grigol's Romanticism was 'more Caucasian,' than its European counterparts. A fact possibly illustrated by the time that other Avar commander, Hadji Murat (1795-1852) - Tolstoy's hero - raided Grigol's home and abducted a Muslim woman. Grigol chased Hadji – apparently only in his underwear – and

40

had the woman returned. This led to that kind of strange rapprochement between enemies often seen in the culturally mixed Caucasus. Two traditional enemies, Christian and Muslim, becoming friends, even going on joint hunting expeditions.

Grigol, although a loyal servant to the Empire, liked to drink with the *karachokheli* (Georgia's poetry-loving craftsmen, who embodied elements of a medieval urban philosophy). During their rebellion (against taxes) in 1865 he first tried to calm them with words. When that failed, the Garrison opened fire. The rebellion ended quickly. But he then wrote to the Emperor asking for leniency toward these poetic guildsmen, explaining they were not properly understood outside Georgia. Eventually he would receive Russia's Order of St Andrew - delivered to him personally by Emperor Alexander II when visiting Tbilisi in September 1872.

So we have two poets. One a famous military uncle; the other his young, more talented, unfamous nephew, who kept begging his elder relative to find him a way out of the civil service. Trapped in his office, Nikoloz complained bitterly that most of his friends were already in prominent positions by the age of 28/29. But Grigol's letters back, although sweet and caring, offered no practical help. Though it might be noted, the letters came from far off in the Baltic States - a bit remote for string-pulling.

But finally Nikoloz received his escape.

His friend Levan Melikishvili was appointed Governor of Nakhichevan Uyezd (now in Azerbaijan), and Tato was hired as his Deputy. Initially the young poet loved the new sights and faces, but it didn't take long to realise, he'd just arrived in one of the Caucasus's remotest backwaters. Soon he began to miss Tbilisi terribly. His enthusiasm for work faded. He started playing cards - and losing. Six months later Levan returned to Tbilisi, dragging Tato back with him, to spare him further gambling debts.

This led to more desperate searches for a new position and Tato's second journey away from home - to Ganja in Azerbaijan with his friend, Mamuka Orbeliani.

But already on a downward spiral, there, as happened all too frequently in those days, illness would suddenly strike. And before anyone knew it, Nikoloz Baratashvili, Georgia's future, greatest Romantic poet,

CHAPTER 3

was no longer of this earth. Some say it was malaria, but whatever the reason, he ended up buried in Ganja, at the meagre age of 27.

Thus his end was wrapped in a tragedy, similar to those doomed Romantic characters he so admired in Byron and Pushkin.

It took a full 50 years for anyone to even consider moving his body back to his beloved native city, Tbilisi.

One reason for this extraordinary fact is that at the time of his death his poetry was still hardly known in Georgia. It would take another major Georgian poet and writer, Ilia Chavchavadze, to right this. But it only happened many years later, after Ilia journeyed up to St Petersburg and visited Ekaterine Chavchavadze's salon – the beautiful wearer of Tato's *Earring'* (then considerably older). One evening she suddenly turned and handed Ilia a hand-written copy of Baratashvili's unpublished poetry.

Bowled-over by what he read, Ilia returned to Tbilisi and began loudly proclaiming Baratashvili as the great poet he truly was – *the* one to give voice to all those impossible ambitions, woes and romantic yearnings of his fellow Georgians. Whose famous poem *Blue Sky* has since become a classic for all those seeking any kind of glimpse of the Sublime. Here is a taster of the first two verses, in free translation:

> *The deep, deep blue, the heavenly blue*
> *place from where all we came and fall*
> *bathed in a radiance divine*
> *my soul pours and pours through love*

> *From a heart whose origins were joy*
> *now a dark and desperate home.*
> *Yet still it flies, soars again*
> *into this deepest of sapphire blues*

Ekaterine Chavchavadze - still elegant in her later years

Chapter 4

Opera

By the mid 1840s the Russians fully controlled all of Georgia. A major invasion hadn't been required, but the last King of Imereti, Solomon II (1772-1815) did put up some resistance, before succumbing (although plotted against them right up to his death). The Russians encountered a people very different in character and spirit to themselves. Unexpectedly perhaps, because Georgians were also Orthodox Christians with their main sacrament as wine – both inside and outside the church. The source of this sacrament, the vine, grew so plentifully in Georgia's warm valleys, a culture of toasting, feasting and story-telling had grown up around it.

Yet regular daily life in Tbilisi was still that of a garrison city. Some even complained it was boring. But around this time the capital suddenly received a new and welcome addition - entertainment.

In fact more than just entertainment, for this modern, European innovation changed the culture of the city forever. This significant addition to Georgian life announced itself in a single building - the new Opera House. One could almost say, a temple to the history of drama trapped in the city walls for centuries, looking for its voice.

For many years Ivane Kereselidze, the editor of the literary magazine *Tsiskari*, enjoyed telling the story of Alexander Dumas, author of *The Three Musketeers*, and his 1859 visit to Tbilisi. How the Frenchman embraced the full range of Georgian hospitality, then proceeded to outdrink his hosts. In *En Caucase*, the book Dumas wrote on his time in Georgia and the region, he claims one of his greatest achievements was to win a local wine-drinking competition.

With a comparable taste for drama as his Georgian friends, Dumas was quick to visit the new Opera House, freshly built in the centre of

44

CHARACTER in Georgia

Tbilisi. In fact, to do it properly he first had his hair cut short, 'Tbilisi style', then visited the sulphur baths, before heading on to the Opera. Although a seasoned traveller of wide cultural experience, he was effusive in his praise – devoting a whole chapter to it in his book, declaring there could hardly be a more suitable setting for any of the world's opera houses;

'I must confess, as soon as I entered the lobby I was astonished by the simple but refined style of its detail... The upper foyer was transformed by Arabic carving and ornament. We entered the hall, which seemed like a fairy-tale palace, due not only to its rich decorations, but also refinement of taste.... I can say without hesitation, never in my entire life have I seen such an enchanting hall... In no way could it be improved.'

Thirty years prior to Dumas' visit, Alexander Pushkin also visited Tbilisi during Russia's campaign to Erzerum in Turkey. Then there was no Opera. The sulphur baths were the city's most operatic feature for the Russian poet, which he praised lavishly in books like *Journey to Arzrum*, – where he immortalised his noseless masseur, Hasana.

Could it be the Opera was a natural evolution of entertainment for such a history-filled, drama-loving country?

If the answer is yes, then we have to thank the presence of a very acute mind – whose idea it was. The new Russian Viceroy Mikhail Vorontsov (1782 – 1856), is still claimed by many as the wisest Russian governor of Georgia (in fact the whole Caucasus). His understanding of the local character, as we shall see later, was beneficial to both nations, but particularly the Georgians.

When Russia added Georgia to its Empire it installed its own administration, albeit into a very different and smaller city to the urbane capital of subsequent years. At the turn of the 19th century, Tbilisi still struggled back to its feet after Agha Mohammad Khan's devastation in 1795 - that razed much of it to the ground. The city was a broken, impoverished, brow-beaten place, though still retaining some of its former charm. The centre was Meidan, around what we now call Erekle's Square. The Russians' first significant building in the shattered city was the Garrison - which included a guardhouse that became used as a prison. It was through the bars of the nearby barracks that the young Grigol Orbeliani - jailed after the failed 1832 plot against the Russian regime - watched the funeral procession of his mother pass by.

CHAPTER 4

Ultimately the Russians began their main architectural developments on the city's then outskirts – what we now call Freedom Square and Rustaveli Avenue. Here they built the Police Administrative building and fountain, then Viceroy's Palace with its large garden.

In those days this land belonged to the noble families – former royals, the Orbelianis, Tsitsishvilis and others. So when the Russian administrators needed land, they purchased it direct from Georgia's nobility.

The ordinary population lived nearer the river in small flat-roofed houses, although today almost no trace of those buildings remain. Then the flat, walkable roof defined this south Caucasian lifestyle. Families could spend a good portion of three seasons on the roofs, often sleeping there.

Tbilisi at that time had few amenities. Due to the steepness of the surrounding hills and violent downpours, the streets could be inundated with floods and dangerous mudslides. A life on the rooftop could even be the safest option; a kind of balcony on the roof. Also it increased the opportunities for social interaction – a hallmark of Georgian life then and now – as well as of course, romantic liaisons.

A popular girl would often insist to her parents that she slept regularly on the roof. Because at night – providing it was starry – admirers could creep up, recite poems, sing songs up at her from the street. This was well described by the German poet Friedrich von Bodenstedt in the 1820s. A unique kind of public courting that continued through to the next century, even when roofs became higher and sloping.

Meanwhile the capital continued to expand steadily.

The place known today as Freedom Square would soon become an enormous bustling, open market, while up the hill, present day's Sololaki existed as a deep, narrow ravine – unsafe during spring and autumn, as floods would regularly carry rocks, tree trunks, dead animals, in furious, tumbling torrent down to the river Mtkvari.

Initially the square was named after Count Ivan Paskevich (1782 – 1856), then, when he took the Armenian capital Yerevan from the Persians, Yerevansky Square. His statue should have been erected in the centre, but in the end never was. But still Yerevan Square could occasionally turn into a heaving water channel for the downhill flash-floods, heading for the river at the point where the Mukhrani Bridge would later be built (today's Baratashvili Bridge).

This area of land and much else beside the river, belonged to the estate of Prince Tsitsishvili - one of the nation's more generous noblemen. When the bridge was built he commissioned the cutting of a road up through the cliff on the other side to connect the bridge to Avlabari - the district above the river's left bank. For many years it was known as Tsitsianov Slope, (today's Baratashvili Rise). He would sell his ravine, road and surrounding land to one Gabriel Tamamshev, a prosperous Armenian merchant. They say the price of the then flat, scrubland was symbolic - two smoked fish and a piece of cloth (enough to make two *chokhas*) – which contains today's Freedom Square.

Interestingly, the merchant didn't want to buy the land at all, but had been convinced to do so by Count Mikhail Vorontsov, our wise Viceroy of the Caucasus, who took office in 1844. As mentioned, a man of vision, who proved to be a very different governor to his predecessors and indeed successors.

Vorontsov arrived in Tbilisi with strong diplomatic and military experience. His childhood and early teens had been spent in London, where his father was Ambassador – (hence why the Russians nicknamed him 'The Englishman'). Very quickly Vorontsov showed himself an outstanding administrator and politician. His flexibility and insight soon launched a more cultural approach to Georgia - its ultimate aim being to steer Georgia's nobility away from political concerns into the cultural.

Many ascribed his actions to a love for Georgia, but others, as a ploy to gain popularity. In either case, Count Vorontsov understood the Georgians well, reporting back to St Petersburg that it was better to have a population as your friend, than in a state of vexatious suppression and rebellion-seeking. Centrepiece of this new policy was his plan for a grand Opera building.

Noticing the Georgian's love of drama and considerable talent for mimicry, Vorontsov set out to create a bold, central venue for the performing arts. At the same time he knew such a project would need back-up, in the form of magazines, newspapers and books in Georgian, so the population could read, write and dramatise daily life in their own language.

Among the supporters of this was the young poet Akaki Tsereteli, who even dedicated a poem to the Viceroy, believing Vorontsov

CHAPTER 4

deliberately misled St Petersburg on Georgia, so he could fulfil his cultural blueprint for the country.

Since Vorontsov had no finances for any of this, he turned to local business, initially approaching the textile merchants to sponsor this grand 'new heart of Tbilisi'. But the traders claimed they'd insufficient means. Then Vorontsov remembered Gabriel Tamamshev. After some persuasion the merchant agreed to finance the project, on conditions the main building also included a caravanserai, with an arcade of shops for retail or rent. Tamamshev knew people would be drawn to the theatre/ opera, and so-doing walk through his rows of shops.

When Tamamshev came to buy the land, only two significant buildings stood anywhere near it; the Police headquarters with its fountain, and the so-called New Caravanserai (today's Art Museum on Pushkin Street), with its imposing, neo-classical façade, completed in 1837. This belonged to another eminent merchant Iakob Zubalashvili, descendant of a wealthy Catholic family.

At this point we might briefly turn attention to this rival building, and the story of Emperor Nikolai I's visit to Georgia in 1837 – the first Russian monarch ever to do so – as the ball in his honour was arranged in Zubalashvili's Caravanserai. At the time it was the biggest building in the city.

As often happens in the Caucasus, the much-anticipated event coincided with a thunderstorm. Because Tbilisi then had no pavements, soon the city was coated in a skin of heavy, sloppy mud. Yet the Emperor's visit was the city's biggest event for years. Everybody wanted to be a part of it, or at the very least, witness his arrival at the ball. Indeed most younger nobles and civil servants shaved off their beards and moustaches simply to copy the monarch's new European style. Elders of course, vehemently resisted.

On the day itself a large crowd of porters gathered at the Caravanserai waiting for the guests: in those days carriages were rare. Most of the ball's invitees arrived in open phaetons, at which moment a porter (usually a furniture remover) would wade through the mud, agree a price, then physically carry the ladies over to the building. A not uncommon sight then in Tbilisi - until pavements arrived.

That day the then Exarch of Georgia (the senior Bishop immediately below the Patriarch, usually a Russian), also attended the ball. Impressed by the building, he inquired if Giorgi, the then late Iakob Zubalashvili's heir, might sell. The Church was looking for a venue for its new centre for religious education. It was this inquiry that eventually led to the establishment of Tbilisi's famous Religious Seminary. Little did the Emperor or anyone know then, future graduates would dedicate themselves, not to a life in the church, but fervent Revolution and a godless Communism. A belief that would not only destroy nearly half the churches of the city, but also wipe out the Russian royal dynasty for ever. The seminary's most famous graduate was of course, Joseph Stalin.

In the end Giorgi Zubalashvili sold part of the building at a subsidised price – the value of its bricks.

Not so far from the New Caravanserai – or to be precise, the exact place where the Lenin monument would later stand (and St George's Column does today) - Tamamshev began constructing the Tbilisi's first ever theatre-opera house.

One can't help but suspect a certain desire to outdo his fellow merchant's building, one hundred metres away. For he invited the young Italian architect Giovanni Scudieri (1817–1851) to design and oversee the work - on the recommendations of Count Vorontsov, who knew his work from his days while Governor of the Odessa region. Scudieri subsequently went on to design Tbilisi's Dry Bridge.

His concept for the giant building was unique for any opera house of the day. He designed it Moorish style, echoing the oriental tradition of the city's vernacular architecture, but with spacious interior rooms set around the auditorium. Unfortunately Scudieri himself died very young, in fact the year the Opera House opened. A heavy block fell on his head while supervising the construction of a military church in the lower Alexander's Garden (today's Alexander Park), near the then Russian army barracks. This church was later demolished when the large Military Cathedral was built in 1871, on today's Rustaveli Avenue. But this grand cathedral also died young, when the Communists pulled it down in 1930, replacing it with the present-day Parliament Building.

The splendid new Opera building finally opened its doors in April 1851 - to a masked ball attended by all of Tbilisi's grandest. The first season officially started with *Lucia di Lammermoor* by Gaetano Donizetti performed by a travelling Italian troupe.

CHAPTER 4

After this, the initial performances were made by a Russian company. But it was Italian opera which the Tbilisi audiences craved. Italian music, Italian composers, Verdi, Bellini, later Puccini… preferably sung by Italian singers. This they felt as a conduit straight back to the cultural heart of modern Europe.

The opera was an instant success and its music quickly spread out into the surrounding, city - at every level. Servant boys could be heard running down streets singing 'Figaro, Figaro…' as the classics rapidly entered salons, dining-rooms and kitchens. *La Donna E Mobile* from Verdi's *Rigoletto* became a favourite with the Tbilisi cobblers. *Tsiskari* magazine reported a peasant woman wearing a traditional headscarf racing into the crowded auditorium saying 'I must hear Bellini!'

It didn't take long for the Opera to be identified as the new city hub, with French fashion shops, florists, haberdasheries, springing up in the surrounding shops. *The* place to meet, chat, exchange ideas, discover what new entertainments were coming to the capital.

Before the arrival of opera, it had been the Georgian table or *supra* serving as the main venue for singing – outside the church. But soon locals from all walks of life were teaching themselves the new Italian arias, as the new kind of pop music. Accomplished Georgian performers began to emerge and significantly, women among them. Thus the Opera launched another small revolution into traditional Georgian society. For until then any career connected with the stage was considered cheap, if not bawdy. Indeed, even in the late 1870s, Mako Saparova (1860-1940), soon to become one of Georgia's most celebrated actresses, was regularly castigated by her grandmother, claiming 'the girl is a disgrace to her family.' The same kind of attitude also extended to women writers, as literature too was considered the exclusive domain of men. This would change dramatically in the 1880s, when women suddenly became, not only well-known writers, but editors too.

As the 800 seat Opera steadily turned into the new beating heart of Tbilisi, long queues would form at the box-office the moment posters arrived announcing an upcoming performance. Sell-outs were too all common and soon under-age school graduates had to be banned from buying tickets. But numerous re-sellers promptly appeared to accommodate the growing market. So military privilege was also dropped and entrance allowed only to those bearing valid tickets.

An engraving of the original Tbilisi Opera from around the time Alexander Dumas praised it so lavishly (in 1859) for its unusual semi-oriental style. It formerly stood right in the city centre in what the Communists subsequently called Lenin Square - today's Freedom Square. After it burnt down in 1874 it stood as a ruin for fifty years, before being rebuilt in today's location up on Rustaveli Avenue.

CHARACTER in Georgia

The building's fabulous auditorium would draw every sort of citizen and nationality. Leo Tolstoy was a frequent visitor. And one of his later literary characters - the Avar rebel commander Hadji Murat (see the previous chapter), also ventured inside. His Tbilisi hosts decided to show him the magnificent new Opera – then the finest building in the Caucasus. But as the only Avar tribesman in the entire audience, clearly recognisable for his large head-piece, the moment the house lights dimmed, someone swore down at him from the upper circle - the Avars were the same clan as Russia's (and Georgia's) greatest Caucasian enemy, the Imam Shamil. Although the precise wording was unclear, Hadji Murat clearly understood the intent of the insult and to save himself quickly fled the darkened theatre. But his rapid exit drew everyone's attention. In the half-light many audience members recognised the North Caucasian warrior, and fearing an invasion, there was soon pandemonium. The lights came back on to a chaotic scene, as people tried to escape in all directions. Maiko Orbeliani, the strikingly beautiful socialite, famously fainted. Thus the only Tbilisi opera Hadji saw turned out to be the one he created himself.

But that was nothing to the première of Verdi's *Il Travatore* in 1857. On this occasion the pandemonium happened outside the building. Huge queues for this highly popular work had formed in front of the booking office. But right on cue, the heavens opened again, sending a flash-flood of water and mud racing down from the Sololaki gorge. Punters suddenly found themselves knee-deep in dangerously fast-flowing sludge and water. Some were lifted off their feet, others fled for their lives to higher ground, or the shelter of nearby buildings. But once the flow subsided, it only took minutes for the re-sellers to appear among the sodden, mud-coated opera fans, to start selling their tickets now at five, sometimes ten times the original price.

Then there was October 1867; the time newspapers were filled with accounts of Giuseppe Garibaldi's heroic revolutionary exploits, which had led to the unification of Italy in 1861. Partly inspired by this, the Opera - being Tbilisi's main public venue - was briefly hi-jacked by a group of nationalist students. They unfurled the Georgian royalist flag in the stalls, began singing their own patriotic songs and anti-Russian slogans. A sentiment echoed in the lines of the Georgian writer, Ilia Chavchavadze's Garibaldian poem - that declared,

53

CHAPTER 4

'I hear that so desired sound
of tearing chains ...
Please let that sound into my country.'

By the time the lights were re-lit, the young patriots had escaped, but their behaviour resulted in a way too heavy-handed response. The authorities promptly banned all Italian opera. The contract with the visiting company was terminated, the Italian singers dismissed. The Russian government obviously decided these Italian emotions were far too similar to those of revolution.

As a result Italy would be elevated to nation of the year across Tbilisi. If you loved Italian opera, you loved Italy, so of course you loved Garibaldi and his struggle against the papacy for a unified Italy. Or so the Russian administrators believed. Certainly the soaring arias couldn't help but echo that instinctive quest for 'freedom' from Russia – as idealised by Georgia's Romantics who part-merged the feeling into the Sublime. Meanwhile the Garibaldi hat became à la mode across the city. Many citizens hung the General's photo on their living-room walls. Stories about Garibaldi's victories and campaigns were repeatedly exchanged across Tbilisi's dinner tables, some true, some exaggerated, some wholly fantastic. But it made any Italian national spotted on the street worthy of pursuing for an earnest conversation.

As for the authorities, they increasingly saw all this as stoking insurrectionist feeling against the Empire. But unwilling to impose a full closure of the highly popular Opera – fearing a backlash - they kept it open, decreeing only Russian operas and performers would be allowed on stage.

The effect was to leave the Opera increasingly side-lined from the city's cultural life. Audience numbers fell. The building became steadily more and more just an entertainment hall.

By then unfortunately, Count Mikhail Vorontsov was long gone from the Caucasus. He'd returned to Odessa in 1853 to die shortly after arrival. But every self-respecting Georgian traveller to Odessa made it their duty to visit his widow and express gratitude for the many far-sighted changes her late husband introduced to their country.

CHARACTER in Georgia

Vorontsov might be held up as the example of an astute politician, whose experience in the Napoleonic and Caucasian wars, then governorship in Odessa, had pre-educated his arrival in Tbilisi. Of the many stories illustrating his understanding of Georgia, perhaps the best, comes during one journey when returning from Kakheti to Tbilisi. On hearing Vorontsov was passing through their lands, locals formed a welcoming chain beside the road, some even following his carriage on horseback. Ignoring his aid's strong exhortations to stop and greet them, Vorontsov merely ordered the carriage to slow, rather than stop. 'These people come from families with a 2,000-year old history,' he noted. 'They don't need anything from us save acknowledgment.'

As attendances at the Opera continued to shrink due to the ban on all things Italian, soon the authorities themselves began missing the full-on melodrama and spark of European opera. Sensing Tbilisi sinking back into its former role as a European backwater, they reversed their decision. Italian opera was suddenly back on. Singers who'd remained in the city, re-exercised their vocal-chords, new companies arrived, and Tbilisi resumed its modern Italian lifestyle.

But just as the Opera's popularity hit new heights – disaster suddenly struck. It happened during a staging of *Norma*, Bellini's 'tragedia liricia', on the 11th of October 1874. In the middle of the performance, thick smoke was seen rising from a small shop adjacent to Tamamshev's Caravanserai. The fire spread rapidly through the many other small shops, then to the Opera itself. A panic ensued and the building was evacuated. Firefighters rushed to the scene from the fire-station right across the street, possessing, so we are told, no more than two buckets for water, two hoses, two axes. Soon the fire was raging out of control, and in a remarkably short time converted to ashes one of Europe's finest and most original buildings. A drama that became a performance in itself – like some terrible finale.

It is said nearly all of Tbilisi's population rushed out to watch their beloved Opera House cry out and die in a furious cadenza of flame. Paradoxically, the nearby fountain in front of the Police Headquarters that might have saved it, that day had broken down. The police summoned every bucket and water-carrier in the city. Volunteers tirelessly fetched water from the river, threw it at the building over the next sixteen hours.

CHAPTER 4

But the flames were too powerful; or to extend the metaphor further, the emotions of the finale performance, way too self-consuming.

As so often happens in Tbilisi, due to neglect, lack of order and then confusion, the catastrophe ran its full course. By morning all the city had left of its finest architectural gem, was a smouldering skeleton.

Luckily there were no casualties – except for the guilty shop owner, who was sentenced to eight years of hard labour.

But the walls of the building survived intact, albeit burnt. The question then arrived – how possibly to restore the Opera to its former glory. Everything was coated in soot; all its finest features gone. The fabulous, 1,000 kilogram chandelier; Grigory Gagarin's superb murals; the magnificent main curtain with its famous depiction of musical instruments, daggers and Russia's introduction of the railway... now cinders.

Despite numerous attempts to perform opera in adjuncts to the broken building, nothing really worked. The many additions and extensions built around it, never looked better than ugly. No proper performances of opera would happen in Tbilisi for the next twenty-two years. The surviving theatre and opera companies re-housed themselves in various buildings across the city, sometimes in specially constructed pavilions. But everyone felt it - the magic of opera could never be the same in the temporary, makeshift venues.

But the city couldn't forget its former glory. Indeed the ruined building stood until 1934, when the remains of the original Opera were demolished on orders from the then Georgian Soviet Socialist Republic's chief, Lavrenti Beria. The square was of course, promptly renamed after him. It might be noted that when he was executed in 1953, Beria Square became Lenin Square, adorned with a large statue of the former Soviet leader - then also safely dead.

Meanwhile back in the late 19th century, the culturally invigorated population of Tbilisi set about constructing a new Opera House, further up what is now Rustaveli Avenue - then Golovin Avenue. The original oriental style of architecture was maintained as also pseudo-Moorish, and much effort put into making the new Tbilisi Opera as grand and enchanting as the first. When completed, and its first season launched in 1896, most agree this was achieved. Indeed today's beautifully stained-glass halls, the Arabian *mashrabiya* designs, marble staircases, still make it one of the world's finest venues for opera and ballet – in its unusual blend of eastern and western motifs and design. And when it too burned down in 1973, it was rebuilt almost identically – as the fine Opera building we see today.

But it should never be forgotten, the rich cultural city that is present-day Tbilisi, grows directly out of that inspired original opera house, constructed into a city dominated by flat-roofed houses, no pavements and serfdom. That its foundations, now long hidden under the swirling Freedom Square traffic, were a vital key ingredient in what has become the modern national character.

Chapter 5

New Times

After years of debate, in 1861 Tsar Alexander II of Russia finally sent out a decree declaring the abolition of serfdom across the Empire – four years before slavery was abolished in America.

But the majority of Georgia's aristocracy found it hard to stomach. For them it seemed like a strange new time. But like it or not, the future was arriving in the Caucasus.

Hearing about the decree, noblemen in Kartli and Kakheti sent a desperate letter to the Russian Emperor entreating him to reconsider. In it they expressed such distress, tragedy and soulful heart-break at the ending of their comfortable regime, it served no more than to reveal how lost and dependent they'd become.

Abolition finally came to Georgia in 1864.

Feeling soon to be deprived of their former lifestyle – which until then aimed mostly at the state of idleness – it dawned they might have to start working for a living. Moreover, if they didn't, the same kind of poverty awaited them as any commoner. Until now their only 'job' had been as serving army officers – with perhaps a bit of professional hunting thrown in. But now, even in the military, a new class of trained officers was emerging – thus stymieing their traditional, pre-set road to employment. Their other option – joining private militia, or voluntary units – offered only a precarious income, especially at times of no war.

Gradually two kinds of nobility began to emerge - those who adapted to the changes, employing a flexibility and firmness of character – and those who didn't, either because they refused to comply, or simply didn't know how. For example, Prince Ivane Malkhaz Andronikashvili, after fighting in the Russian-Turkish war, showed himself a shrewd and wealthy nobleman. When asked how he managed to accumulate such riches and expand his estate, he laughed saying 'I spent thirty years building it brick-by-brick, but am still far from finished.' He then noted that his neighbour 'has spent the same thirty years destroying his, and isn't finished either.'

With the full abolition of serfdom, some noble families quickly became impoverished, but others, like Prince Andronikashvili, flourished. Amongst the former set, perhaps the most miserable were the lower-rank nobility who spent their lives doing the bidding of their more senior lords, without any need to show initiative. Too often their worlds simply collapsed.

An illustration came in the fashion among noblemen in Western Georgia to display long, well-preserved fingernails. Their tragedy was immortalised in Davit Kldiashvili's stories, particularly his prose piece, *Autumn Nobility*. Long manicured fingernails implied you never had to do physical work, the righteousness of your position meaning that others - like serfs - did it for you. But with emancipation it wasn't long before society started to look down on those whose only life achievement was their fingernails.

Then there was that other sign of status - the front gardens of the Imeretian nobles. Ideally, these would display a mature oak tree, gracing the centre of a well-kept lawn. The older and bigger the tree, the more impressive the family lineage - so they thought people believed. Furthermore, it gave excellent shade in the summer. So noblemen could happily recline for hours under these splendid leafy canopies, basking in the appearance of absolute proof of who they were.

Except that in these new times, appearances were no longer enough. Without access to proper and regular income, the nobility discovered that even owning a decent pair of leather boots might require earning them.

And frustration at these changes went right to the top. Once, during his election to the Board of the National Bank, Grigol Orbeliani – a highly educated nobleman - was heard saying: 'The trouble with our country began when I, grandson of King Erekle, was given the same number of votes as Tsalkalamanidze (which in Georgian means 'Mr One Shoe's son'), a commoner – one!' Although in fact he was also nobility, just a lesser kind.

The old-guard couldn't restrain their irritation at low-ranking nobility, e.g. children of clergy, being appointed to key positions.

CHAPTER 5

'Whenever you go to a newspaper office now, all you see are clergymen's sons. How on earth can you talk to them?' was a typical complaint.

And just as bad; this new middle-class seemed more inclined towards education - that truly devious method of social climbing.

The already mentioned Grigol Orbeliani was appalled at this one-man-one-vote system of electing the first Chair of the National Bank. 'How can we install a mere vassal of the Sumbatashvili estate?' he exclaimed. Even if the man in question was Dimitri Kipiani (1814–1887), already one of Georgia's most esteemed, 19th century public figures, as first head of the Nobility Bank.

It was also the time when a thieving nobleman suddenly became just a thief; and a nobleman who killed someone, just a murderer.

As for true Revolutionaries – Georgia's aristocracy was less tainted by them than Russia's. The Decembrist revolt of 1825 St Petersburg, never seriously crossed the Caucasus. One reason for this was that dissent usually fomented in and around European university life, and Georgia then, had no such institutions. Even as late as the 1880s, Kutaisi prison held only two Revolutionaries – Giorgi Laskhishvili (future editor of *Iveria* newspaper) and Giorgi Zdanovich (possibly a relative of the two Futurist Zdanevich brothers who discovered the painter Niko Pirosmani). As for noblemen, also only two – Paata Goshua from the western province of Samegrelo - serving time for murder - and Giorgi Mikeladze, a former Convoy officer turned highwayman. His is another good example of noble demise.

In his younger days he served in the Emperor's military escort, like many Georgian aristocrats. An easy posting with little more to do than shooting practice, horse-riding and chit-chatting. But on his return from St Petersburg, with no post awaiting back home as formerly, he chose the only profession that seemed to match his training – highway robbery. But lacking the skill and intelligence of someone like Arsena (see Chapter 2), he soon became well-known. Way too well known. It didn't take long for officers of the Empire to hunt down this embarrassment to their alumni. He was arrested then locked away for years in Kutaisi prison, while endlessly bemoaning his personal tragedy.

Fortunately the highwayman option wasn't popular. Most noblemen who failed to adapt simply wasted their lives away drinking, taking loans they couldn't repay, and finally selling their family estates. One such was

CHARACTER in Georgia

Prince Giorgi Machabeli who without really trying, squandered away his wealth to zero. Not a bad person really; simply not knowing any better. Having married the daughter of a wealthy Tbilisi merchant, he merely went out and lived his noble life. Then mysteriously it was all gone. His fate was typical of many a failed aristocrat, dying ignominiously in an inn near Gori. Adding insult to injury, when his family arrived to take the body home, the inn-keeper refused to release it without payment of his long-accumulated credit account.

We might note that Giorgi was father of Ivane Machabeli (1854–1898), a significant intellectual of his time – see Chapter 7.

One person who wrote a book describing the Georgians of that period was Vasily Velichko (1860–1904), a nationalist Russian playwright, minor poet, and editor of *Kavkaz*, a semi-official gazette written in Russian. He liked the Georgians, but in a vaguely condescending, imperial way. For instance, he maintained that Georgia didn't need universities, only military colleges. He declared that Georgians were excellent warriors, reliable friends, good officers - but that was all. Perhaps he also entertained suspicions of that middle-class social climbing technique - education.

His book *The Caucasus* might prove interesting even today, despite his chauvinism. Velichko hated Armenians, criticised them unremittingly, heightening it via his praise for their neighbours, the Georgians. The contemporary poet Akaki Tsereteli disliked this about him, claiming Velichko deliberately set the nations against each other, merely to make himself look clever.

Velichko once encountered Akaki and Ilia Chavchavadze at a dinner. Knowing that neither were then on speaking terms, he proposed a toast in verse, wishing 'the two Georgian titans' a noble reconciliation. As was his style, Ilia rarely made pronouncements at such gatherings, so just listened and smiled. Akaki however, the more outspoken of the two, suddenly lost his temper, saying to Velichko: 'Our disagreement is none of your business. And just so you know, we both dislike Russians!'

Vasily Velichko put the decline of Georgia's nobility purely down to excessive drinking. He also claimed that the moment they stepped out of their homeland they transformed, became well-organised and civil. But once back across the border, they reverted to their old ways of wasting time and energy on wine and feasting.

CHAPTER 5

True, the Georgians could certainly drink, some taking it better than others. However, in the nobility's case, the consequences were more pronounced. With their background of no responsibility and if possible, idleness, all too many descended straight into the arms of alcoholic dependence.

And the place most of these indolent noblemen found themselves washed up, was Tbilisi. As previously wealthy and daring, now impoverished and useless, a good number were former military officers - like Leo Andronikashvili, and his friends, Kola Baratashvili and Kola Ratishvili. They'd rendezvous in an inn, drink enough glasses to put them in the mood for a good fight, then set about finding the right person. Just about anyone would do – save perhaps the *karakhocheli* (the gilded craftsmen recognised by their black *chokhas* – cartridge-belted coats). To cap off the evening, an inebriated nobleman might ask porters to carry a table down the street while he danced on top. Or for a laugh they'd push a horse-drawn city tram off its rails - like the great heroes they were. Nor of course, could they forget their guns – former emblems of their trade. One favourite practise was a kind of dance that involved waving pistols while shooting ecstatically in the air, as and when the spirit moved them. And sometimes not just in the air.

So much bounteous energy that could have been applied into countless productive activities, just pouring itself literally, down the drain. All that military acumen and training, frittered away into empty partying night after night. The kind of confused laziness depicted by Ilia Chavchavadze in his character Luarsab Tatkaridze (see Chapter 1) - effectively turning nobles into glorified, middle-class tramps, living minute to minute in a state of pure self-obsession, deliberately self-blind to political events.

But to leave our portrait of Georgia's changing nobility with Luarsab, would be to do them, and the country, a disservice. Because, as hinted earlier, some of them adapted unexpectedly well.

Ilia Chavchavadze, 'that liberal round ball,' father of the modern Georgian nation

Chapter 6

Ilia - Father of a Nation

As already said, literature played a major role in the development of 19th century Georgia. And when it comes to the next stage in the national character's evolution, one writer stands head and shoulders above the others.

Which is why he had to be assassinated.

Rotund, of average height, likeable in appearance and unhurried in his manners - is how Ilia Chavchavadze (1837-1907) came across to his contemporaries. Or - as the poet and decorated General, Grigol Orbeliani (1804-1883) once joked, 'that liberal, round ball.'

Although most memoirs present similar portraits of Ilia as a highly influential public figure, there was nothing comic about him. For on the inside, 'the ball' was seen as a representative of all things wise and considered by the vast majority of Georgia's population.

Neither did his face, expression nor mannerisms, give much away. One of his contemporaries said, 'seeing all of Ilia's photos didn't mean you knew what he looked like.' He talked slowly, rather monotonously, unemotionally, lacking the impetuosity and drama of his fellows – to make this one of his defining characteristics.

Ilia's eyes were his most striking feature, always slightly jovial but connecting straight down to his other, most prominent trait – his words. People claimed that in an argument, he was more or less unbeatable.

Ilia Chavchavadze is often described as Georgia's prime cultural innovator for over half a century, possibly the country's most influential writer and 'the father of our nation,' - by which is meant modern independent Georgia. He often joked about the epithet, saying if he fathered the whole nation, who was left to father his own children? Which in the end, perhaps ironically, he never had - much to his regret.

CHARACTER in Georgia

He gained this title because he wasn't only a man of eminent words, but unlike many wordsmiths, he knew how to put them to use. His declared aim was to build and promote a new sense of Georgian identity, as unique and distinct from others (like Russian). This, against the backdrop of the large neighbour's attempt to assimilate Georgia into its Empire. His ultimate goal was full Georgian independence.

Aided by, and sometimes competing with, his fellow poet Akaki Tsereteli, in addition to writing his highly popular articles, stories, poems – like *Is He a Human*? (see Chapter 1), *The Hermit, The Ghost, Traveller's Notes'*, he started a number of important clubs and societies, two very popular publications - *Sakartvelos Moambe'* (1863–1877) 'The Georgian Messenger' - and *Iveria* (1877–1905). He created Georgia's first small public museum, and founded the Bank of Transcaucasia (called The Nobility Bank). In fact, nearly all accoutrements needed to sculpt a people's new idea about themselves then inspire these beliefs into action. Ilia's fans claim he was the man most responsible for modern Georgian's concept of their new nationhood.

Some have called him a nationalist, but he was far more subtle and artistic than this, though still taking his lead from the great liberal political movements emerging in 19th century Russia and Europe. His thoughts aligned with modern ideas of self-government; social, human and women's rights; socially concerned economics and education, and the establishment of a civil society. But these also included his accommodation with the Georgian Orthodox church and language rights for fellow Georgians – with the formation of his *Society for the Spreading of Literacy Among Georgians*. His ideas became mainstream in Georgia during his lifetime, and his popularity crossed into all levels of society, even within the Russian authorities, so that at the end of his life he even served in the upper house of the first Russian State Council in St Petersburg.

His presence is etched so deeply into Georgian history that even as late as 1987, when the Soviet Union started collapsing and Georgia's sense of independence leapt back to front stage, Ilia once again became man of the moment. He was canonised by the Georgian Orthodox Church, as St Ilia the Righteous. Georgia is one of the few countries to make a secular writer into a saint.

One theory holds that his early liberal ideas, expounded in essays, stories and articles, when mixed in with his political actions, served as

CHAPTER 6

the foundation stone of Georgia's later Social Democratic (Menshevik) identity, which would set up the independent Georgian state between 1918-21.

Of course the Social Democrats hotly denied this, only once ever saying anything good about Ilia - when standing over his coffin. The prominent Social Democrat, Karlo Chkheidze, grudgingly admitted that some of his early stories had been 'socially accurate.'

As committed Marxists and atheists, forging what they saw as their own new Socialist identity, the Mensheviks accused Ilia of being a bourgeois, old-fashioned aristocrat and Capitalist banker to boot. In return Ilia once described Noe Jordania (1868-1953) - who would later lead the Social Democratic state - as 'Marx's blindfolded parrot.'

Towards the end of his life the Social Democrats even initiated a campaign against him, their newspapers declaring him a rich and callous landlord. They claimed he denied peasants access to spring water on his land; would stand on his balcony in expensive furs ordering their clay water-pots to be smashed.

Ilia reacted to such ridiculous accusations only once, saying he'd never owned a fur coat, and remained baffled why they were so suck on such a bizarre subject.

As for the spring water, in fact his neighbours were always free to use it. He simply asked they not break-into his land through the fence, but walk around and use the gate. However, being true independently minded Georgians, they preferred the short cut.

Neither was Ilia rich – contrary to many opinions. His main income came from the Nobility Bank, which set him in the upper-middle-class bracket. Only later in life did he gain a significant salary - while serving as a member of the State Council in St Petersburg.

As for the cruel landlord... He had no property in Tbilisi until the last year of his life, always staying with his sister. His main base, the estate in Saguramo (home of today's Chavchavadze Museum) actually belonged to his wife, Olga Guramishvili (1842-1927). His own family inheritance was a modest house in Kvareli, Kakheti. His enemies (he had plenty) claimed he only married Olga for her money. Again not true, for after Ilia's death it transpired that Olga also had very little - only the property. After the Communists came to power in 1921, they made very sure his widow lived out the rest of her life in poverty.

Saint Ilia the Righteous

So what was it that made this rotund writer and activist so widely loved, then hated by the Social Democrats, so as to end up butchered by assassins?

First, we might say his steadiness of character and wit, which almost everyone found hard to resist. There were many anecdotes. Like the one with a man called Khachaturov, editor of the Russian newspaper *Tifliski Listok*, ('Tbilisi Pages'), who remarked he'd heard that Ilia's mother was Armenian, which might explain why he was so clever. Ilia replied he was amazed that Khachaturov was so stupid, when both his parents were from Armenia.

We might make a note here about the complexity of nationality and religion in the Caucasus - then and now. Priests would often insist that both partners should be of the same religion before marriage – and require conversions. Or else conversions would be done for commercial reasons, as in the case of Ilia's mother (originally Georgian), who converted to the

Armenian, Gregorian church – meaning she didn't become 'Armenian,' merely followed their faith. In a similar way Georgian Catholics were often called 'French,' and all Muslims 'Tartars.'

Second, and more importantly, we must look to Ilia's main achievement - his Georgian language magazine *Iveria*. At first just a weekly, *Iveria* would become the single most influential organ in Georgian society, both culturally and politically - for several decades. It picked up on all new innovations and ideas; discussed and promoted art and culture, always with an independence-orientated slant. Many writers, later hailed as doyens of Georgian literature, had their first works either published or promoted in *Iveria* - such as the poet Vazha Pshavela (1861-1915) and Alexandre Kazbegi. Indeed Vazha even worked at *Iveria*, although his employment lasted only three days – fired for writing poetry instead of working (translating news from Russian to Georgian). He became so bored that finally, instead of handing-in his latest translation, he dropped the poem he composed that day on his editor's desk – his resignation put into verse.

But before Ilia Chavchavadze began publishing *Iveria*, he cut his publishing teeth on a smaller publication, *The Georgian Messenger*. This monthly part-inspired the creation of the Georgian-language daily newspaper *Droeba'* ('The Times'), whose most celebrated editor was Sergei Meskhi (1845-1883). It may be worth looking more closely at *Droeba* as it would become the template for *Iveria*, which replaced it.

Droeba's office was in the so-called 'New City' – the open space beside today's upper Rustaveli Avenue - sometimes called Republic Square. The New City and its many fine buildings, was later razed to the ground by the Communists to create a flat parade arena. The paper inhabited the top floor of a building opposite - the still surviving, domed, Art Nouveau mansion built by Melik-Azariants. *Droeba's* office building was also flattened to make way for the grand Academy of Science building, which still stands - although its once famous sports shop 'Dynamo,' is gone.

Droeba's office looked for all purposes, like a family home. It even functioned like one. A Georgian-language newspaper demanded the same courage and gruelling hours from its staff, as any family. It included all the same sibling-esque rivalries - for minimal financial reward. Both it and *Iveria* soon turned into kind of clubs, or free hotels for like-minded activists, who came and went bearing food and drink, some even living there full time - like the writer Alexandre Kazbegi (1848-1890) who'd nowhere else to go. Yet outside the door both papers provided that vital, day-to-day life-blood of keeping the population informed on local and international events. But with a low-print-run, operated almost single-handedly, *Droeba,* offered only a selection of the news, its column-inches further restricted by its role as campaigning voice for various Georgian independence factions. Also it competed with a number of well-financed, professionally run Russian-language papers, with wide readerships – also employing liberal journalists. It might be noted that by 1905 Tbilisi, then the largest city in the Caucasus, had 19 Russian language newspapers; 10 Armenian; 6 Georgian; 2 Azeri, and 1 German.

Initially the bulk of *Droeba's* articles were republished straight from the Russian. Its press was housed in the same apartment as its offices, where the typesetters - mostly poorly educated - also doubled as the paper's editors. Aristocratic readers criticised both *Droeba* and *Iveria's* deliberate use of simple language – to make the articles accessible – and dubbed the journalists 'clergyman's sons.' Although almost none were.

But in those days, merely making it to print in Georgian, was an achievement.

The previously mentioned Russian nationalist, Vasily Velichko, was one of the many advocating the full eradication of the Georgian language. 'What's its point, when charcoal vendors run around shouting 'ougli, ougli!' ('ougli' is the Russian for coal)?' he asked.

Children were already being punished for speaking Georgian in schools, and the idea being floated of banning Georgian chants and liturgy in church services. Velichko suggested his Georgian colleagues should instead merely translate a 'proper' Russian newspaper.

But it was precisely this existential threat to Georgia's language, the sense it may be wiped out for all time, that became *Iveria's* rallying cry when it took over from *Droeba.* Ilia used this to the paper's big advantage, realising the population craved a good, sharp-eyed instrument written in their own language, to keep them informed, awake and primed.

Which it did extremely well, and right under the nose of the Tsarist censors.

Due to the revolutionary ideas spreading like wild fire across Russia and Europe, every newspaper, magazine and book across the

CHAPTER 6

Empire required vetting before publication. This involved another pre-printing by the presses, and signing off.

Fortunately for Georgia, the chief censor was for a while Rapheal Eristavi (1824-1901), a friend of the liberals, and author of several highly patriotic plays and poems. Journalists saw him as a mild, thoughtful censor, often turning a blind eye. Once Giorgi Laskhishvili (1866-1931) – a future Socialist-Federalist revolutionary, who later became editor of *Iveria* - recalled his fury when Eristavi deleted a passage from the Bible in an article. Eristavi said he did it purely to protect the author from the clergy – who'd sue at the drop of a hat. Laskhishvili later admitted he was glad for the cut. Ironically perhaps, because when it came time for Ilia Chavchavadze's *Iveria* to be forcibly shut down, it was due to the actions of indignant church officials when Laskhishvili was Editor.

But this official purification of literature could also be very severe. The censor before Eristavi was one Luka Isarlishvili (1814-1893) who Russified his name to Isarlov. When the novelist Alexandre Kazbegi was about to publish his first book, Isarlov returned it to the author with the text 90% deleted. A furious Kazbegi went ahead and printed the book anyway. But three days after publication he had to watch the entire print-run seized, then burnt to ashes.

As a result Isarlov often had to deal with young, hot-blooded, anti-Russian liberals brandishing daggers, pistols - or bribes. But his more sympathetic successor, Rapheal Eristavi, only struck out 'dangerous' passages – simply because he didn't want to see their only Georgian language newspaper closed down. In his heart Eristavi was a great Georgian patriot and widely loved by the intelligentsia.

When *Droeba* was closed down - on a direct order from the Viceroy, in 1885 - Ilia and Georgia's liberal journalists had to develop a metaphoric language, requiring, so they thought, true sophistication to decode. Sometimes it worked, but other times, clearly not metaphoric enough. *Droeba's* closure came via a seemingly harmless satirical feature depicting a mullah and a *qadi* – an Islamic judge. But a Western Georgia governor decided the *qadi* was a thinly disguised a version of himself, so sued the paper for defamation. Coincidentally, another satirical article by Ivane Machabeli (see Chapter 7) also appeared, this time depicting a rude and drunken Russian workman. But a Cavalry General called A. M. Dondukov-Korsakov – well known for loving the bottle – believed the drunkard deliberate caricatured himself. Needless to say the court sided with the Governor and General.

As years passed writers began to perfect what they called an AESOP (after Aesop's Fables) language, a sophisticated code of double meaning able to by-pass the key words that would shut down their paper. One publication that perfected this to a fine art was the satirical magazine *Eshmakis Matrakhis* ('Devil's Whip') which criticised everyone and survived from the turn of the 20th century right up to the end of the Menshevik period.

Immediately after *Droeba* closed a group of ten, led by Ilia Chavchavadze, gathered urgently in a Sololaki flat in Tbilisi. The nation was now without any Georgian-language daily paper, so they decided to transform Ilia's weekly magazine *Iveria* into a daily, with Ilia as Editor-in-chief.

But once up and running, the troubles continued. As the Revolutionaries became more active, Georgian society increasingly polarised (some would say, not unlike today). Personal and ideological rivalry between newspapers in all languages, raged ever more fiercely. Failing to follow the accepted direction of your particular paper usually meant losing your job. And 'direction' was usually synonymous with ideology. On one occasion a fierce disagreement between Ilia and fellow liberal writer Niko Nikoladze seemed resolvable only by the death of one party. Ilia had flatly refused to make any changes after Nikoladze criticised his paper's direction, saying he'd defend his choices to the death. To show his commitment, very uncharacteristically, he challenged Nikoladze to a duel. Although it never happened, it indicates the level of passion swirling inside the blood of fellow activists.

Part of the anger - or was it rivalry - came as a result of Ilia Chavchavadze's appointment as a regional civil judge in Dusheti, just north of Tbilisi – a position he held for nearly three years. This made him superficially 'establishment.' And while away from the capital, Ilia sensed Nikoladze using the opportunity to twist the paper away from his own, less radical thinking, to his own.

In a way they were all eccentrics, and excellent journalists. But publishing a paper demanded devotion and sensitivity to all nuances of social change and the ever-adjusting politics. And some were definitely more alert than others. While Ilia excelled in this, Ivane Kereselidze

CHAPTER 6

(1829-1892) editor of *'Tsiskari'* magazine between 1857-1875, once received a barrage of complaints from Georgian students studying in Russia, on 'the direction' he'd chosen for his publication. So to rectify this he simply switched its northward delivery route - from overland, to the sea.

Was he really that unconscious of his own point of view? Most believed this the case, and another example of the entrenched political ignorance of some old-guard editors – the kind of intransigence Ilia and his colleagues had to face every day from the Russian establishment.

But intransigence belonged to both sides, and often originated in areas other than ideology. One example comes from Anton Purtseladze (1839-1913), a critic and novelist working for *Iveria*. As another thinker fully willing to back up his ideas with bullets (he even once even fired at Nikoladze - although missed), he once invited colleagues home for a meal and a reading of his latest article – criticising Shakespeare's use of a ghost in *Hamlet*. He claimed it dated the play to the pre-Francis Bacon era (he thought of himself as a 'Baconist'), and not 'modern enough.' But the food arrived late and the host soon found himself being yelled at for his 'stupid ideas' – which as soon as the meal arrived, became peacefully debated again. This shows very clearly how hidden, apparently unrelated emotions (in this case hunger), all too often haunt intellectual discourse and politics.

As the years passed Ilia became less of an editor, writing only occasionally for *Iveria* – around a dozen articles a year. His work at the Nobility Bank and *Society for the Spreading of Literacy Among Georgians* came to dominate.

Privately he was known to dislike feasts, visiting people, going to the theatre or opera. Fundamentally a quiet person, shunning large gatherings, reluctant to talk in public or propose toasts at parties – where he would sit quietly, smiling and listening, usually not drinking.

Except for two days a year.

The first was his wife, Olga's birthday, which doubled as a New Year's celebration, where any close friend could show up to the dinner, without invitation.

The second was his personal day in Saguramo, the 20th July, which later became known as Iliaoba, and is still celebrated today in Kakheti – due to his Kakhetian origins (usually in August). This took the form of a giant communal party.

CHARACTER in Georgia

The Iliaoba event required mammoth organisation, and the burden fell mostly on Olga – as the intellectual Ilia, simply wasn't up to it. 300 plus guests could easily arrive, mostly from Tbilisi. Livestock had to be slaughtered, hundreds of litres of wine gathered, and countless other details prepared. The event attracted all the neighbouring nobility, liberals from Tbilisi, Ilia's personal friends, peasants from Saguramo, students from the agricultural college and countless others.

For this one day the whole estate would transform, teeming with human life. Peasants would be seen singing in one corner, groups of Tbilisi pipers in another, noblemen with their guitars in another, a group of dancers here, wrestling competitions there, all lasting well into the night.

As for Ilia's impracticality re running his estate; this ultimately counted against him. He employed bailiffs, including several corrupt ones. Indeed it is believed that one of them, named Jashi, was part of the assassination plot – although he was cleared in court.

To make up for his domestic failings, Ilia liked to read Russian papers and magazines devoted to agriculture - believing that agrarian reform as important as the political. Marvelling at new technological inventions, he would sometimes purchase them – in many cases only to see them lie rusting in sheds, because neither he nor his peasants could understand the instructions.

One such was the 'chicken incubator,' which try as they all might, nobody could figure out. It failed to work and all the chickens died.

But when Ilia sat down to write, he became disciplined to the point of obsession. He locked himself in the study with a mountain of *papirose* cigarettes, smoked and wrote determinedly, sleeping on the sofa, if sleeping at all. The only person allowed to enter the room was Olga, and only carrying food or tea. When he emerged he'd deliver his work (often long essays), to his younger editors telling them 'to check its tooth' – meaning making it sharp enough. He always listened attentively to their critiques.

Back in Tbilisi local politics continued to hot-up. Particularly when three students from the Theological Seminary (who all later became liberal journalists) spotted the Russian Viceroy to Georgia strolling in the Alexander Garden. Instead of taking off their hats, or rising to their feet and bowing, they sniggered ostentatiously.

CHAPTER 6

This particular Viceroy was the Grand Duke Mikhail Nikolaevich (1832-1909), the brother of Tsar Alexander II.

Not one to tolerate sniggerers.

Indeed in his 20 years in Tbilisi (or Tiflis as it was then called), he oversaw the abolition of serfdom and a new building boom in the city, including the splendid new Viceroy's holiday residences in Borjomi, near Likani.

The three students were promptly arrested for disrespect, which in turn led to a radical purge of the Seminary – with many students expelled. But as is so often the case, one over-reaction only generated another. The hard-line, anti-Georgian Rector of the Tiflis Theological Seminary, Pavel Chudetsky, ramped up his dislike of the Georgian liturgy; started describing it as 'in a dog's language.'

So on the 24th of May 1886, one of the expelled students, Ioseb Laghiashvili - a character straight out of Dostoyevsky – ambushed and stabbed the Rector. He died from the wounds.

Infuriated by the crime, the then Russian Exarch promptly delivered a sermon in Tbilisi's Sioni Cathedral unashamedly cursing the Georgian nation. The local nobility and high society just listened on in silence. Only one public figure took it upon himself to defend the country – Dimitri Kipiani (1814-1887), a journalist, lawyer and statesman – by sending the Exarch a letter asking him to please retract his diatribe.

But Kipiani's bravery only resulted in a yet more animosity and an intense dislike of him by the authorities, especially the acting Governor Dondukov-Korsakov, who would later have Kipiani exiled to Stavropol, where he was killed - apparently by robbers, some say to order.

As for Ioseb Laghiashvili himself, he was tried and convicted, but spared death due to his youth. After spending many years in a labour camp, he was eventually released and made his way to San Francisco to become, some say, the first ever official Georgian émigré to the USA, achieving American citizenship. He also kept in close touch with Georgia's Revolutionaries back home, such as Pilipe Makharadze (1863-1941) and the Menshevik Noe Jordania.

Back in his Tbilisi office Ilia often employed young journalists and graduates from the Seminary, preferably those who'd fought against the Empire's mission of Russification. One such was Giorgi Laskhishvili (later *Iveria's* Editor-in-Chief) who'd served time in Siberia for participating in the Odessa student protests. Gradually Laskhishvili lured other radicals into the offices, which soon became a kind of hub of dissent, with its spines spreading out to the farthest corners of Georgia.

Because Tbilisi still had no university, many of Georgia's liberal journalists and activists received their education at the Theological Seminary - then the country's main seat of higher learning. And it has to be said, only a fine line divided these activists from hard-core Revolutionaries. Perhaps the main difference was that in Georgia they opted to fight the system more within its legal framework – while in Russia their contemporaries reverted to terrorism – eventually assassinating Tsar Alexander II.

This more nuanced rebellion might be illustrated by the writer Niko Nikoladze who once recalled meeting his tearful, royalist father after he heard about the death of Nicholas I. The death of a monarch transcended the usual political boundaries, partly because in Georgia, royalists wanted to restore their own monarchy - itself a form of rebellion against the Russian state, which had abolished it.

In his memoirs Giorgi Laskhishvili's recalls the day when Ilia Chavchavadze heard the news that his paper *Iveria* had to close. Again clerics at the Theological Seminary lay behind it. A series of critical articles by the young journalist writing under the pseudonym, Ia Ekaladze, (roughly translated as 'violet thorn') so enraged the clergy they demanded the Viceroy immediately shut down the paper. Having been looking for an excuse – he did. But a year and a half later Ilia managed to skilfully resurrect *Iveria* under a different editor, Alexandre Sarajishvili (1851-1914).

As for moments of relaxation from his many missions - Ilia would play cards or backgammon. In his excellent memoirs of those times, Ekvtime Takaishvili expresses a curiosity why Ilia, a man indifferent to gambling, always seemed to win. And why Akaki Tsereteli, who played far more often, invariably lost. In the end he assumed that Ilia, true to his more well-balanced nature, chose only those games that could be analysed and counted. But that Akaki loved the drama of endless, extravagant risk-taking.

And this circumspection also showed in Ilia's ability to negotiate a path through awkward situations – as when Tedo Sakhokia (1868-1956), a well-known ethnographer, lexicographer and translator – published a

CHAPTER 6

collection of Akaki Tsereteli's 'jokes' - or so he claimed. *Iveria* promptly trounced the publication as pure frivolity – claiming the jokes had little to do with Akaki, merely exploited his name. The review was so convincing nobody purchased the book. Facing financial loss Sakhokia chose to sue *Iveria* for libel.

But on this occasion Ilia opted to defend the paper himself – and won the case easily. His technique was to read out the book's bad jokes in a disbelieving tone to the court, until the judge begged him to stop.

Later Ilia told Sakhokia that most people enjoyed Akaki Tsereteli's jokes, including himself, and he was only trying to save Sakhokia's reputation from being dragged down into the gutter by such an 'unworthy of him' publication.

It should also be noted that Akaki was an excellent editor himself. There is the story of a Georgian Colonel - Ivane Kvinitadze - arriving at *Droeba* with a pile of terrible poems, insisting they were published. Akaki apparently took one look, declared them 'wonderful' and promised to print them 'soon.' Sitting right next to him was another genuinely good young poet, whose poems he'd just turned down, with a caveat, 'fix them and bring them back.'

'Why did you reject me and accept that idiot?' the young poet declared. Akaki replied, 'I get bad poets out the door as fast as possible; and tell the good ones to work harder.'

When *Iveria's* door finally had to shut permanently in the autumn of 1906, by then other Georgian language publications had already sprouted, up to 15 in Tbilisi alone – which includes the unofficial ones. *Kvali'* ('The Trace') was one such - where Akaki Tsereteli and Ivane Machabeli were often published. Indeed *Kvali* published Akaki's highly popular, patriotic poem *Gantiadi* ('The Sunrise'), though not long after that, it too had to close.

Meanwhile editorial boards were already being taken over by a more revolutionary younger generation, like Noe Jordania, although at that point was still in prison in Russia.

One of Ilia's closest friends was Davit Sarajashvili (1848 – 1910). As founder of a chain of brandy factories across the Russian Empire, unusually for someone of great wealth, he genuinely cared about the conditions of his workers. This led him toward a more Socialist approach to business – and interestingly, Noe Jordania. He would help sustain

Jordania while in exile, keeping him in funds, especially during his Italy years.

But as Georgian politics heated up again, there came the single, terrible event that everybody feared for years, but nobody believed would actually happen – until it happened.

Ilia's brutal assassination on the 12th September 1907.

After the failed 1905 Revolution attempt in St Petersburg, an increasingly heated, revolutionary atmosphere began to propagate across the Southern Caucasus. Political murder was more and more frequent. That day Ilia was returning home from Tbilisi to Saguramo, when an armed group jumped out of the bushes and stopped the carriage. As they raised their weapons, Ilia stood up and shouted,

'Don't shoot, I am Ilia!'

With his identity confirmed the armed men promptly shot him through the head. After this they murdered his bodyguard, battered his wife Olga and ransacked the bodies, as if to imply a robbery.

Which it wasn't.

The event sent shock waves, not only across Georgia, but Russia too. Some claim this event as the final nail in the coffin for the 1905 Revolution.

It inspired reams of articles and analysis. The entire Georgian population discussed it. The great poet Galaktion Tabidze (1892-1959) wrote a poem, beginning with the words

'When Ilia was killed in Tsitsamuri
With him died an epoch.'

Ilia's friend Vazha Pshavela noted grimly, 'Ilia's murderers would have killed all of Georgia if they could.'

As for why, and on whose orders - there are many theories. Some suggest the Bolsheviks - who made no bones about hating him. Others that this may have been the only time Georgia's Mensheviks and Bolsheviks worked together (although this seems unlikely because such decisions were usually made by Revolutionary Committees, and the two Marxist parties had already separated in 1903). In the extensive and very formal investigation all the killers were identified save one, who until this day is just called 'someone from Imereti,' which probably means a Party man with a mission. The coachman was implicated and hanged, along with the three others - in spite of Olga's pleas to spare their lives.

CHAPTER 6

The only surviving murderer, Grigol Berbichashvili, initially fled, possibly to Iran. But after the Bolshevik take-over in 1921, decided to return to Georgia. Arriving in Tbilisi he headed straight to the nearest Communist office declaring,

'*I* am the killer of Ilia Chavchavadze... and with this hand. Give me a pension!'

It's not known if he received it; but he somehow survived on until 1937, when he was suddenly arrested, charged with the murder and executed (along with a lot of others that terrible year). This was only because Ilia had suddenly been resurrected by Stalin on the jubilee of his birth. Ilia museums were opened, books published and a new investigation ordered, pointing, surprise, surprise, to *Okhranka* involvement (the Tsarist secret police). It coincided with the time Moscow celebrated the 'Georgian Cultural Decade,' also initiated by Stalin. This included the resurrection of poets like Nikoloz Baratashvili and Vazha Pshavela - though Stalin couldn't understand all the fuss about Vazha. 'He's so narrow-minded,' he once remarked after WWII. This one comment meant no more editions of Vazha until after Stalin's death in 1953.

As for Ilia, so many editions of his writing have appeared since then, that even the Communist leaders came to grudgingly admit him as 'the spiritual father of 19th century Georgia.' Thus the 'father of our nation' slogan would come to stick.

And it's continued sticking on into the 21st century.

Iakob Gogebashvili

Chapter 7

The Mother Tongue

There's something about obsessive-compulsive behaviour that fits well with the process of writing – so people say. The need to find exactly the right word for precisely that feeling or event. Often it just won't let you go. And this can easily extend off the page.

Take the day the poet Akaki Tsereteli witnessed his friend and fellow writer Iakob Gogebashvili (1840-1912) walking rather oddly down the street. He took five steps in a straight line, stopped, took another five directly sideways, stopped, then took five more straight again. The highly curious Akaki eventually concluded Gogebashvili was avoiding puddles, but in such a meticulous way as to prevent contact with even the smallest amount of water.

The reason… it seemed that wet feet, so Iakob later explained, was the first step toward respiratory illness, which of course could be terminal.

But Iakob Gogebashvili had good reason to look after himself. He'd become author of a book soon to become essential to Georgia's future generations, and for years to come - *Deda Ena* ('Mother Tongue'). One of the best-selling Georgian books of all time. The goal of this work, indeed his whole life, intended that children and their children's children, continued to speak the Georgian language well enough to maintain it as a first-class literary instrument. For it certainly was until then. As Professor Donald Rayfield of Queen Mary's University, London noted in his compendium of *The Literature of Georgia,* - until the time of Shakespeare, Georgian had as rich a literary history and as many users, as English.

Gogebashvili realised that for Georgian identity to maintain a steady course into the future, children required a definitive, class-room text book. And his obsessive attention to detail certainly helped, when it comes language training.

'*Deda Ena,*' first published in 1876, would prove an excellent tool for exactly this. It was reprinted into countless editions over the next hundred years, and also used as a template for many other Caucasian languages. Most, if not all of Georgia's native speakers were, and often still are, brought up on its evolving editions. It begins with an introduction to the Georgian alphabet, then captures the child's interest via catchy quotes and illustrations from literature - including Shota Rustaveli. These are well-chosen and tend to stick in children's minds, even on into adulthood. He augmented his textbooks by writing fairy tales, poems and various pieces of historical fiction. His second major work was *Bunebis Kari* ('Gate to Nature'), a kind of children's encyclopaedia - evolved the process further. It too became massively popular.

But all this work required good health, and Iakob's hypochondria would become legendary among his friends. The butt of numerous jokes. Indeed Ilia Chavchavadze once asked his colleagues not to show Iakob any new medical books, because he'd soon be suffering from every illness they depicted.

To stay safe, in the heat of summer Iakob Gogebashvili used to wear rubber overshoes on top of his footwear. Designed normally to protect shoes during times of heavy snow or rain - to wear them in Tbilisi's shimmering July and August, was peculiar to say the least. Though of course Iakob wasn't only protecting his shoes – but also his mind. Though he himself wouldn't see it that way. He remained convinced that wet feet could all too easily instigate a chain of rapidly deteriorating illnesses, resulting in probable death.

But he did have one excuse for his eccentricity. In childhood he'd been diagnosed with tuberculosis. To combat its ever-present threat his parents initiated a rigid regime of lifestyle-control – and successfully held the disease in check. He merely continued the routines into adulthood, and with even more vigour. While many tittered behind their hands, he never modified his behaviour. Even gained respect for his doggedness.

In fact Iakob's personality wasn't really the kind people felt the urge to mock openly. His fastidiousness was integral to his curious but likeable character. The discipline of maintaining good health, he said, applied to all

CHAPTER 7

aspects of life. Once he claimed, 'If anyone goes to the same lengths as me with tuberculosis, they can live with this disease indefinitely.'

Another part of his precautionary technique was not to marry, thus eliminating any chances of infection from close contact; also from passing the illness onto a wife or children. But some historians claim this was merely an excuse for a deep-seated bachelorhood - which insisted on 100% control of his day. Additionally, without a family to support, he gained a certain financial independence - unlike his fellow writers. And it has to be acknowledged, in his case the many techniques seemed to work, at least to some degree, for even in his 70s people said he looked unusually well-preserved.

Thus he was able to live out a simple, ordered life - which most writers require anyway. He maintained only two real interests – children's books and bodily health.

Initially he'd been a teacher; having received an education at the religious seminaries of Gori, Tbilisi, Kiev – then also at Kiev University. He returned to Tbilisi in 1863 and taught mathematics and geography at the seminary there, before being dismissed in 1874 for allowing the topics of his classes to stray into the forbidden areas of art and politics. So he merely made his own house up in Mtatsminda, a centre for such discussions to continue.

His punctuality was another oddity for a Georgian – his compatriots not being renowned for their timeliness. But Iakob would leave his house at midday sharp every day, walk down the slope into town, carry out his various tasks carefully one by one, then return home at the stroke of four, for dinner. After that he worked till late into the evening.

Interestingly his writings contain many detailed descriptions of his family village – Variani – even though he never visited again after his teenage years. The reason – 'too windy.' And there was a marsh nearby. Even though he clearly loved it. On the occasions he needed to visit his relatives, he invited them to the comparative safety of nearby Gori – which had a hospital.

In fact he declared only two towns in all of Georgia safe enough to visit - the spa resort Borjomi and the well-forested town Surami, both known for their clean, pine scented air. Meanwhile he endlessly consulted medical books and numerous doctors – though ultimately only ever fully trusting one - his loyal friend, Dr Tite Kikodze. This was mainly because the doctor was happy to drop everything when summoned by Iakob, then travel to whichever resort the writer chosen for his elaborate regime of treatments.

When not writing books, letters and articles Gogebashvili devoted a good amount of time to Ilia Chavchavadze's *Society for the Spreading of Literacy Among Georgians*. As part of this he helped create a bookshop on what is today's Rustaveli Avenue. He saw the shop as another key element in the process of maintaining Georgian culture – and encouraged it to function more as a club, with numerous literary events, social and educational gatherings.

Though when attending these, Iakob had to be particularly careful. Zakaria Chichinadze, the literary critic and publisher, once described how Gogebashvili made his entrance to the shop. First he pushed the shop door open a crack, then shouted in through the gap, 'Close all the windows!' Because any small draught he felt, might disturb the balance of his body and trigger an infection.

One can easily imagine the smiles; especially as Tbilisi's streets were, and still are, notoriously windy. People did report sightings of a hunched figure wrapped in a thick shawl, scuttling down the avenues, quickly ducking into doorways during strong gusts.

As for his personality, in all matters, save health and work, Iakob came across as quiet, attentive and generous. He paid for a number of his relative's education and volunteered in several local schools. But when, in 1881, Georgia's conservative Education Inspector, Kirill Yanovsky (1823-1902), announced a ban on all Georgian language instruction in schools, Iakob's character abruptly transformed. He became enraged in a single-minded, even vindictive manner, proceeding to hound the Inspector relentlessly and at every opportunity. He was so dogged that even Yanovsky eventually found himself having to give in. For like a modern-day Cerberus, Gogebashvili guarded the national language with every fighting limb he possessed.

And they came back into play whenever regulations limiting the use of Georgian re-appeared. Gogebashvili would bombard the Imperial ministries with letters and complaints, assiduously quoting back their own guidelines - having carefully studied their wording. On nearly all occasions his protests were accepted and Yanovsky would receive

CHAPTER 7

instructions from St Petersburg to reverse his edicts. This would prove very significant for the language's long-term preservation - preventing the usual, slow, insidious creep of eradication.

As for his books *Deda Ena* and then *Bunebis Kari*, both required constant reprinting and updates – and in increasing numbers. This in turn demanded long sessions of proof-reading, which Gogebashvili insisted on overseeing himself. For each of his books had to be flawless.

He would only allow a select few to attempt the job, one of them being the then Tbilisi Mayor, Vasil Cherkezishvili (1858-1910). Gogebashvili declared he had a 'good eye,' but was 'too slow,' due to his official duties - which Iakob considered very subordinate to his own mission.

He also wrote and printed children's books – such as his story, '*Two Stubborn Goats.*' This tells the tale of two intransigent goats who meet on a narrow bridge. Since neither would even consider giving way, they simply head-butted each other until both fell into the water. A story, as we shall see, with plenty of real-life parallels in Gogebashvili's Georgia.

For relaxation Iakob would drink small quantities of red wine, for its health-giving qualities only. Not white if he could help it. But once at a farewell party he became famously drunk. After breaking several glasses he had to be carried home - apparently tightly clutching his wallet, lest anyone steal it. But even in the state of inebriation, his own clumsiness infuriated him. On arrival he was summarily undressed and put to bed. But in the morning he woke up furious again. For his rescuers had seriously endangered his life - by removing his socks.

Then there was the time Gogebashvili required a new home-help. He spent hours interviewing candidate after candidate, fearing any one could be a thief. Like many Georgians he kept large amounts of money hidden at home. His publisher, Ivane Avalishvili recalled the time he delivered Gogebashvili's royalties in gold coins – witnessed by the servant. Iakob had suddenly shouted, 'Why have you brought these here? They're not mine. Take them away!' As soon as the servant left the room, Gogebashvili reprimanded Avalishvili sternly, locking the coins away in a drawer.

The same went for his relations with women. As a true educator and polymath, he always welcomed visitors at home. Many came for consultation, particularly on topics like the Bible, mathematics, and of course, teaching methodology. His home - high up the hill in Mtatsminda (1 Khevi Street) where he believed the air cleaner - became a haven for discussion groups, sometimes radical, although he was never a great fan of the Russian Revolutionaries and remained faithfully Georgian Orthodox. Then people started noticing a single young woman visiting in the evenings and increasingly regularly. The servant had to summon her carriage later and later each time - until the day Iakob realised people were noticing. Apparently he announced rather too bluntly, 'I'm afraid I have no intention of marrying. And because this city is so small, our meetings have to end.'

Clearly he feared not only gossip, but losing his perfectly maintained state of emotional independence.

Ultimately it wasn't his lungs, but intestinal cancer that called him in. And quite quickly. Sensing the approach of death, Iakob meticulously checked then re-checked his will, noting down the name of every *Society for the Spreading of Literacy Among Georgians*, employee. When finally all was in order, he died more or less as he had lived, in a carefully arranged way, with all his affairs laid out neatly for the future.

A unique man, in a unique time. When people's eccentricities were far more accepted and put to good use, than they are today.

Chapter 8

Shakespeare's People

The main purpose of literary fiction they say, is to help people define how they see the world – and themselves. That of its many methods of delivery, theatre is probably the most potent - where lines and catchphrases stick quickly in the mind and then grow wings.

For instance, mention the writer Ivane Machabeli (1854-1898) in Georgia, and the name of an Englishman immediately springs to mind – William Shakespeare (1564-1616). The Elizabethan playwright's plays had been circling the globe since the 17th century. By the 20th most nations had their own versions of *Romeo and Juliet, Hamlet, Macbeth, King Lear, A Midsummer Night's Dream.*

For this we have to thank Shakespeare's many talented translators - of which Machabeli was certainly Georgia's finest.

So is it a coincidence that Machabeli's life itself would come to resemble that of a Shakespearian tragedy? The translator of the highly popular *Hamlet* in Georgia, would have his own

'too too solid flesh…
melt thaw and resolve itself into a dew'

in a way that nobody has been able to fully decipher.

The mystery of Ivane Machabeli's early death, or rather disappearance, remains unsolved to this day. A drama in itself, haunting the nation's literary history in the same way the voice of *Hamlet's* ghost lingers under the play's every scene. The man who created Georgia's finest translations of *Hamlet, Othello, Macbeth, Richard III, Julius Caesar, Antony and Cleopatra, Coriolanus, King Lear,* ' simply vanished off the face of the earth like a dew in his 40s, leaving no physical trace.

But the legacy he left in the Caucasian air was enormous. Right up to the present his translations of Shakespeare's plays are regarded as the closest to the original in spirit and meaning. They are usually the ones performed by the Rustaveli, Marjanishvili and Tumanishvili theatres, home and abroad. Other translations came – at least four more *Hamlets* – and mostly went. But his stayed. A few have had their wording slightly modernised from Machabeli's 19th century vernacular. But thanks to Ivane's inspired translations, Georgia saw a surge in popular theatre and amateur dramatics back in the 1870s and 80s. This became the foundation stone on which the country built its current reputation as a highly cultured, theatrically-accomplished nation. It is said modern Georgia is one of the few nations to consistently impress the English with Shakespeare. When in 1980 the Rustaveli Theatre brought their musical, almost burlesque version of *Richard III* to the Roundhouse in London, it created a sensation – and gives another clue to the national character. With the ending of the Soviet Union, this one production would spawn a host of other touring Georgian productions, first in the UK, then around the world. It would also inspire the urge in many people to visit Georgia.

So why did Shakespeare suddenly become so popular in Georgia?

Apart from the obvious quality of the poetry, plot and characters; it might be remembered that in mid 19th century Georgia, political speeches in Georgian language were forbidden. The mother tongue was under serious pressure. The Russian Empire even sought to abolish the Georgian language gospels – due to the Tsar's very realistic fears of a nationalist rebellion. Some of the Georgian revolutionaries, many of whom were writers as we have seen, believed the great Shakespearean themes – hunger for power, revenge, love, hubris - could be used as a subtle vehicle for dissent, *Richard III* and *King Lear,* being two prime examples. So to air them not only in Georgia, but in the Georgian language as well...

This sentiment was not missed in any way by Ivane Machabeli.

It is said that the first-ever performance of Shakespeare in Georgia happened in the Mingrelian market village of Bandza, at the start of the 1870s - *The Merchant of Venice*, translated by Dimitri Kipiani. A time when village theatre was a very new idea in Georgia. But it picked up speed rapidly in the 1880s – as we shall see in Chapter 11.

CHAPTER 8

As for the engine behind such national popularity? Ivane's own literary life may be a good example. It first developed out of his interest in language, in turn spawned from his childhood love of singing, mostly in church, and its accompanying strong religious feeling. By the age of six he was not only an accomplished reader of the Georgian language, but also the medieval script of the Georgian psalm book. Many scholars, Akaki Tsereteli among them, would come to the church in his home village at Samachablo, Tamarasheni, in the area the Soviets renamed South Ossetia - to hear him chanting the Georgian liturgical psalms.

But this facility was then put through the pressure-hose of difficult teenage and early adulthood years. These stemmed mostly from his family estate's financial struggle, thanks to the debt-mountain accumulated by a spendthrift father. This, added to the fact his mother was of poor health, spending much of her time ill. Thus the family burden fell on the shoulders of his elder brother Vaso, who more-or-less brought up Ivane (who was technically a Prince) – while constantly having to chase off creditors like his uncles - who demanded their house and property for debt repayment.

Ivane's love of foreign languages – the source of most information for Georgians - soon became irrepressible. Soon he became accomplished not only in Russian, but English, German, French, Italian, Spanish, and Latin, refining his knowledge constantly all his life. It was helped by periods of study in St Petersburg, Germany and France. The British scholar and fellow linguist Marjory Wardrop - who translated *The Man in the Panther Skin* by Shota Rustaveli - asked for his help while translating her *Life of St. Nino*. Later, after his disappearance, Marjory even suspected Ivane may have snuck away into the land of Shakespeare, and initiated a search for him back in Kent.

Meanwhile his family's financial predicament meant his unique literary abilities had to play second fiddle to the necessities of economic survival, in his case as full-time employment. He could only indulge his great love - the translation of literature - in his few pockets of free time, even though at the age of 23, he was once declared the country's most talented young professional.

Finally, it was Ilia Chavchavadze who put Ivane's considerable abilities to proper use. They met by accident in Saint Petersburg where Ivane was studying and had set up a popular Georgian theatre circle.

They then worked together on the first-ever Georgian *King Lear*. Ivane translated it from the English, which Ilia then put into verse. It was first printed in 1873, then remade as a separate book in 1877.

This collaboration led to more, then the eventual establishment of a famous literary triangle in Georgia, which lasted nearly twenty years.

The triangle's three corners were about as prestigious as they could then get in Georgia; Ivane Machabeli, Ilia Chavchavadze and the poet Akaki Tsereteli. Initially it stood solidly enough. Committed friendships all round. But steadily two of the three began to bicker, then argue, eventually to rage against each other. Ivane and Ilia's promising beginnings descended into a strong-willed and irreversible animosity. The triangle only survived because Akaki and Ivane remained staunch friends, as did Ilia and Akaki – though with a few famous gaps.

It was Akaki who last saw the talented translator alive – which has led to plenty of speculation in the rumour hungry nation. The drama of this literary love triangle kept the whole country on their toes, resulting in a number of fantastic theories explaining Ivane's bizarre disappearance after midnight on the 26th June 1898, at the meagre age of 45.

Before further investigating this mystery we need to look at these three complex and intertwined human beings.

After their inaugural collaboration on *King Lear*, Ilia Chavchavadze took Ivane under his wing, offering him a modest position in his Nobility Bank. But due to his precocious talents, Ivane soon ended up as its Director.

The Bank found itself being run by two, wilful, independent, literary talents. Some would say, never a good formula.

Initially, due to his eminent practicality and intelligence, Machabeli flourished – as he would have in any business. A fast and efficient decision-maker with exceptional memory, he would learn tasks quickly, then innovate. It is said that if Ivane read a book in the morning, he'd be the subject's expert by evening – able to quote back long passages, verbatim.

Added to this was the fact that 1880s Tbilisi offered few entertainment opportunities for its population, apart from opera and a smattering of local theatres – like today's Griboyedov Theatre near Freedom Square (originally called Nobility Theatre Hall).

Since just about anything connected to the Nobility Bank had implications for the whole country, the Bank's Board Meetings – always open to the public - soon became a sought-after event, like a form of entertainment.

CHAPTER 8

This is partly explained by Georgia's role as a vassal state of Russia. It had no parliament, so no government debates and dramas for the press to sink their teeth into and splash across front pages. Thus the Bank's Board meetings were added to Tbilisi's entertainment calendar – which grew significantly in popularity as rumours circulated of the animosity between its Chairman, Ilia Chavchavadze, and Director, Ivane Machabeli. Slowly this professional disagreement evolved into a personality wrestling match, observed by the nation. A kind of tragi-comic, Shakespearian soap opera, whose main literary point seemed to reveal just how easily close friendships can develop into open war – to be cemented into place by the presence of an audience.

Though they themselves didn't see it that way.

Eventually, due to the Board Meetings' swelling number of drama-addicted observers, a new venue had to be found. And was it coincidence this turned out to be a theatre?

Soon these popular dramas had most of Tbilisi on the edge of their seats (the papers covered them religiously) and dividing into two camps; supporters of Ilia and the Bank executives - and fans of the opposition leader, Machabeli. A factionalism playing out again and again in Georgian politics (and theatres) ever since. Needless to say, stories of epic battles were soon gossip-inflated out of all proportion, along with the number of supporters for each side.

Although an engaging pastime for the general public, the conflict inevitably damaged both parties, and indirectly Georgia itself. Probably Machabeli suffered the more, because he lacked Ilia's ability to restrain his emotion. During these increasingly public arguments, Ilia usually remained calm, speaking thoughtfully and logically, while Machabeli often exploded. On some occasions he even ran out of meetings arm-waving and shouting. At which point his supporters could even rush the stage brandishing revolvers.

Shakespeare couldn't have written a better quarrel scene.

Indeed some say that Georgia's instinctive love of drama, both on and off the stage, explains why the country has proved itself, again and again, to be so accomplished with its many touring theatre productions. More recently, when the Tbilisi's Marjanishvili theatre took *As You Like It* to London's Globe theatre in 2012, the Georgian version turned out so popular, the production was invited back, then toured Europe.

CHARACTER in Georgia

Ilia Chavchavadze and Ivane Machabeli during friendly times

Eventually Ivane Machabeli abandoned the Bank and all work connected to his now enemy, Ilia Chavchavadze. But while he never suffered any shortage of alternative job offers, the conflict deeply affected him. Especially because in all their battles, Ilia always came across as the cool one.

An example of this is when Sergei Meskhi, the owner and editor of *Droeba* - then the only Georgian language daily newspaper - became ill and needed suddenly to sell. Because the paper also came with debts, Ilia Chavchavadze stood out as the best candidate to take on ownership – having access to funds.

Although by then Machabeli had already distanced himself from Ilia, his proved literary talent and linguistic reach, positioned him as the logical choice for editor. Thus he went ahead and announced the fact the world.

So of course, it didn't happen.

CHAPTER 8

When Ilia secured the money and paper, he promptly hired someone called Kananov as editor – who nobody knew and many doubted even spoke Georgian.

Not long afterwards Machabeli suddenly and unexpectedly found himself in the position of being able to buy a failing *'Droeba'*. He promptly did so, making himself editor. Naturally he used the paper's column inches to lambaste Ilia – which only re-kindled the war.

But the tables then turned again, when *Droeba* faced abrupt closure by the censors in 1885, with Ivane still at the helm. This left the only Georgian language publication as the weekly newspaper – *Iveria* - which promptly took over the much needed daily-paper slot. And who became its editor... Ilia Chavchavadze.

There are many such stories illustrating the surreal rivalry between these two supremely confident, uncompromising human beings.

As for the effects of all this on the Bank's staff and clients; generally they found Machabeli more amenable, and Ilia the tougher one.

As did Prince Shalikashvili – granted a loan by the Bank for the purpose of agricultural development at his estate in south Georgia. Machabeli believed in the Prince's intention to re-cultivate – especially when set against the many insincere grant requests from other failing, indebted aristocrats. So when the Prince's repayments slowed, Machabeli extended the loan. But shortly afterwards, while Ivane was actually away on summer holiday, he was suddenly confronted by a distraught Shalikashvili telling him that Ilia had sold his entire estate from under his feet. Or as Shylock put it in *The Merchant of Venice,*

> *"You take my life,*
> *When you do take the means whereby I live!"*

Chavchavadze justified his action by saying he disbelieved the Prince; that the investment's lack of progress demanded the lands be turned over to those better able to manage them.

As a result Ilia Chavchavadze was often accused of being a hard man, selling land on to foreigners, Armenian merchants and Russian officials – at the expense of Georgia's natural-born owners.

But Machabeli went further, describing Ilia as cruel – as the time when a member of the Georgian Literacy Society died. His family lacked funds for a funeral, so the Society appealed to the Bank's Board for help – which required a meeting at short-notice in Ilia Chavchavadze's house. But hearing that Ivane would attend, Ilia refused the request, declaring Machabeli would 'never ever' cross his threshold. Thus the meeting was held in the Society office - without Ilia.

Such events mounted up and would haunt Machabeli to the end of his life - deepening the mystery of his disappearance. Some have speculated he had moments of profound self-doubt - as expressed by Shakespeare's *Richard III* - so well translated by Ivane.

> *'What do I fear? Myself?*
> *There's none else by.*
> *Richard loves Richard;*
> *that is, I and I.*
> *Is there a murderer here?*
> *No. Yes, I am.*
> *Then fly! What, from myself?*
> *Great reason why:*
> *Lest I revenge. What, myself upon myself?'*

In truth nobody knows for sure when Ivane died – the date of 1898 is simply the year he stepped out of sight from Georgian society and the world.

The drama was compounded by the fact Machabeli's body was never found - although painstakingly hunted. Ivane lived near the river Mtkvari and a night watchman reported he'd seen him walking toward it in the early hours. So for many days, rafts and boats searched up and down its banks, the long hooks pulling out all kinds of surprises - but never Ivane.

In turn this led to Akaki Tsereteli's much reported 'jokes' about Ivane's departure. The first suggested that Ilia Chavchavadze should stand on the Metekhi Bridge, or join the searchers in their boats, because for sure Machabeli would appear, unable to resist the chance to confront his rival.

The second was that if Ilia mingled among the bridge's crowds, if Machabeli did surface from the river, he'd promptly submerge again, to avoid him.

Such enthusiastic poor taste points the finger again at the third member of this dramatist's triangle – Akaki Tsereteli. Much older than

CHAPTER 8

Machabeli - like Ilia - he became Ivane's devoted friend and confidante, due partly to his non-partisan, purely poetic interest in the Bank's affairs. Akaki, a great raconteur and gossip-lover, would describe Machabeli to his many hosts (he loved to couch-surf around Tbilisi's noble households), as one of the finest public figures Georgia ever possessed. As for Akaki's own personality, people joked he only befriended doctors, women and children. But he remained probably Georgia's most discussed character during his lifetime – a true celebrity. Generally he remained loyal to those he considered friends and via his charm managed to get away with his no-holds-barred jokes. Books of his jokes began to appear all over town, some without his knowledge, making him joke again about, 'Just how many Akakis do we have in Georgia?'

Probably his most internationally famous poem is *Suliko*, which became a song sung all over the Russian, then Soviet Empire. It's usually thought of as a man pining for his love Suliko. But it also puns on the Georgian word for 'soul' – *sul,* and even found itself later used as a woman's and a man's name. Akaki described poetry as 'the trumpet of the earth,' and his most loved poem is *Dawn* - both a lament for the writer and statesman Dimitri Kipiani (who also translated Shakespeare) and an allegory for the quest for Georgia's independence. Its first lines go,

Oh deep blue sky,
oh emerald land
whose soul
puts the soul in me
I'm so yours
so fully
that even after my death,
I'll grieve for you
always

Meanwhile, the productions of Shakespeare truly took off in Georgia – helped by the construction of what later became the Rustaveli Theatre (1887). Machabeli's translations enabled some truly memorable performances to become known across the Russian Empire. In the Tsarist period, Lado Meskhishvili (1857-1920) acquired fame as *the* legendary *Hamlet* and *Lear* on numerous stages. A Shakespearian actor delivering the old-school tragedies, full force. The same tradition carried on into the Soviet period – it was hard to censor Shakespeare. Towards its end, the great Ramaz Chkhikvadze took his *Richard III* and *King Lear* onto many international stages, giving a certain poignancy to memories of the Stalin/Beria era terror. The power of his performance alone put Georgia on the international map, and inspired many of its first post-Soviet visitors.

Some claim that the high quality of Georgian theatre played a role in the unusual amount of political attention the nation has gained since its 1991 independence. A love of dramatic poignancy perhaps...?

But there's another ingredient to Machabeli's own personal mystery play - his wife Taso. Nee Bagrationi-Davitishvili (1869-1917), her father, Alexandre, hailed from one of the branches of the Georgian royal family, and was significantly rich, with two sons, and three well-taken-care-of daughters.

To understand the full complexity of the triangle, it's worth glancing at Taso's younger years. Akaki often visited the house, so knew Taso well, right through her girlhood. Furthermore, she was also the same age as his son. Akaki never hid the fact that he always loved Taso dearly, claiming her as a kind of ideal in his life, and a unique human being.

But was there more here than meets the eye?

Some people have since asked: was Akaki the kind of man to help a friend marry his own lover? Did he really have more than platonic eyes for this under-age girl he'd known from her early childhood?

Added to this was the ingredient of Akaki's fame. He commanded huge attention, trust and national love. People would gather on railway platforms just to catch a glimpse of the poet sitting in the train.

So, one might also ask, where in all this was Akaki's own family?

Answer; far away in St Petersburg with his Russian wife Natalia, leaving Akaki alone and fancy free, being hosted all around Tbilisi by his many friends and admirers.

Asking these questions in his memoirs, the politician Ivane Zurabashvili (1872-1940) chatted with a number of contemporary women about Akaki's romantic life, without naming them of course. It seemed the poet unquestionably enjoyed female company – of all generations. Conversation, everybody said, was his great talent and enjoyment. But was it his greatest pleasure? The women claimed it was, that he never exceeded the bounds of lavish flirtation. Some also declared – how could they possibly consider him as a mere lover, when he belonged to Georgia's immortal literary pantheon?

Zurabashvili also interviewed Taso Machabeli, and although he did not disclose her identity, it shines through. She claimed her relationship with Akaki was always that of attentive personal assistant – which she officially became. She would diligently look after everyday affairs and later his personal health. Nothing more.

From the tone of the memoirs Taso comes across as believable.

However, their relationship is ripe with indicators and symbols pointing other directions. For instance, Akaki once wrote a short story *She,* where the narrator meets two women while in the countryside, falls in love with one, but because she is too young, the feeling remains platonic. The protagonist then urges his younger friend, Achabeteli, to marry her, promising to become their eternal friend - like a father or elder brother. Some believe Achabeteli should be renamed Machabeli. They also suggest that if Akaki wanted to keep an affair with Taso secret, why write such a story?

So in the real world, was Akaki instrumental in their marriage?

Difficult to say. Ivane was certainly a quick decision-maker, with a good instinct for character. After his first meeting with Taso, they quickly met a second time for a two-hour walk. That evening Machabeli sent a relative over to the hotel where Taso stayed with her sisters, bearing his marriage proposal. Apparently the request came accompanied by a copy of Akaki's new book – which could have been more than symbolic.

Then there were the poems among Akaki's 15 volumes of work, which he dedicated to Taso. But of course, he dedicated poems to others too.

One more twist in the story is Akaki's preference for staying with the couple during his many Tbilisi visits. Ivane and Taso owned a house on present-day Kostava Street, where it still exists - opposite the lower entrance to Vera Park. When buying it Ivane wrote to Akaki in St Petersburg, praising its charms. The small back garden; its many plants; the table placed there specifically for Akaki to enjoy his summer evenings (another Shakespeare scholar, Niko Kiasashvili, preserved Machabeli's dining table at Tbilisi State University). The letter was extremely warm and included much love from Taso. And there are many other such letters.

Coincidentally, it was at the same table that Akaki and Ivane played backgammon on the evening of Ivane's disappearance, a time when Ivane still recuperated from an illness that required the partial removal of two ribs. The military surgeon had performed a successful operation, probably saving his life.

Did this illness have any bearing on his disappearance?

All these questions remain unanswered.

Meanwhile all around them the 19th century was nearing its end, amidst an increasingly heated political atmosphere and *'aritatsia i propaganda'* (a term invented by the Communists to describe deliberate political agitation). While Ilia Chavchavadze stood at their vanguard, Machabeli was less politically active – a fact probably assisted when the Russian Viceroy closed-down *Droeba*.

But Ivane had no shortage of work. After leaving the Bank he carpet-bagged across many of Georgia's leading companies and offices, achieving senior positions. During this time he managed to also translate some Molière and Goldoni. Yet as with any of Georgia's late Romantic-era writers, Ivane's own formative romantic life can't be ignored either.

At the beginning of his career he was motivated, if not completely inspired, by a deep love for Mako Saparova, one of Georgia's then most outstanding actresses. He sat down and translated *Romeo and Juliet* specifically for her – with a personal dedication (though it seems his version has since either been lost or was never completed).

No doubt at all that for him then, his feelings would have been well-articulated by Romeo himself,

'O, she doth teach the torches to burn bright.'

But unfortunately for Ivane, she went on to marry her fellow actor Vaso Abashidze. But the Shakespearian torch had been lit.

Machabeli was forced to declare his failed first-love as one of those great learning lessons of human tragedy, so well articulated in his *Romeo and Juliet.*

'Love is a smoke rais'd with the fume of sighs;
Being purg'd, a fire sparkling in a lover's eyes;
Being vex'd, a sea nourish'd with lovers' tears:

CHAPTER 8

What is it else? a madness most discreet,
A choking gall and a preserving sweet.'
Similar niceties around the emotion also applied to Akaki
Tsereteli, who dearly loved his Russian wife Natalia Bazilewskaya –
although for much of their marriage they lived at different ends of the
Russian Empire. He often complained that when together, she suffered
that overpowering need to nurture, which ended up trying to control
him, especially in matters of health. But Akaki maintained his love for
her by re-assigning this guardian's role to the fussings of his sister back
down in Georgia, thus leaving Natalia's over-protectiveness safely out
of reach.

After Machabeli's disappearance, Akaki lived for sixteen more
years, Taso eighteen. In those years Taso and Akaki exchanged letters
when Akaki was away in St Petersburg. But they revealed little more
than the standard expressions of affection. Gossip-hounds believe there
was another, unpublished, or 'hidden' correspondence. But no such thing
was ever found, which leaves it doubtful. Akaki usually addressed her as
'Dear sister' or 'Princess', nothing more. But neither was Ivane's widow
an easy person – coming across in the letters as fastidious, sometimes
even severe. Certainly she did a great deal to help the ageing Akaki. He
had plenty of debts and often needed to travel for health reasons. Taso
helped with all this, as a genuinely devoted friend.

People have speculated too about possible family tensions. A
tight-fisted, sometimes harsh Taso; an explosive Ivane, living in the same
house. Then again, every family develops its many private mechanisms
of restraint not seen by outsiders.

As for the evening Machabeli disappeared; he said he felt weak
after his operation and impatient at the slowness of his convalescence.
He and Akaki had sat round the table playing backgammon, while
Taso sewed. Then they all went to bed without eating a proper supper.
Apparently Akaki slept on the living room sofa.

In the morning Ivane was gone – for ever.

It didn't take long for the whole city to know Akaki had stayed
that night with the couple. He gave a detailed description to the police,
including an account of hearing something in the house around midnight,
possibly a cat. But he then went back to sleep.

At the time Akaki was 60, Taso – 30 and Ivane – 45.

So would a man of a respectable age like Akaki, involve himself in such a fraught and dangerous affair? True, as a poet he thrived on drama and entertainment, but it seems most unlikely he'd dive body and soul into the world of cheap novels, at this time in life.

However, that didn't stop the gossip – of which there seemed no end. One reason could be that the police investigation was never fully revealed and analysed, in the way it was after Ilia Chavchavadze's assassination nine years later – which became almost public property. Machabeli's disappearance is still wrapped in Elsinorian mists (*Hamlet*'s castle) and Akaki's version of events, mostly gospel.

The more wicked rumours had it that Akaki killed Machabeli – accidentally. There was speculation later from Machabeli's servant about a brick factory near Machabeli's house – with its high-temperature, bone-consuming, kilns. Also the report from the night watchman who'd seen Machabeli in the street and asked if all was OK. Machabeli apparently said nothing.

Most today believe Akaki's involvement remains highly doubtful. But whatever the truth, Machabeli's disappearance continues to haunt Georgian literary history like a phantom, echoing to the sounds of his explosive character, charm, hard life and Georgia's many superb Shakespeare productions.

Perhaps it is this, the physical ghost of language and phraseology, that is the real phantom left behind.

When his life and body evaporated from the earth, his poor mother believed he'd run away abroad to Argentina. In England Marjory Wardrop thought he'd pilgrimaged Shakespeare's way. Others in Tbilisi speculated he'd joined a group of travelling gypsies.

Was any of this really possible in such a complex and brilliant man? His was a life filled with the speeches and poetry of William Shakespeare, which he would consider, analyse and re-make into Georgian while walking down the streets of Tbilisi.

Did he possess the impulses of one like Prospero, who finally chose to live far away in a cell, as in *The Tempest*? Was he like Gloucester in *King Lear*, who in a fit of depression declared,

"This world I do renounce...!"

CHAPTER 8

Or, like the tragedy generated by *Romeo and Juliet*'s warring houses, the Montagues and Capulets, did the conflict between himself and Ilia Chavchavadze, end up in death?

Like all great dramas performed on any kind of stage, these events have been left for future generations to ponder, clap, and then if the Zeitgeist allows, use for their own personal edification.

Vazha Pshavela wearing a papakhi hat posing for a family portrait on the threshold of his Chargali home in Pshavi. The woman standing immediately to his right is his second wife, Tamar. The gap beside his left shoulder originally contained his elder brother Levan - who was subsequently shot by the Communists in 1923 (one among 93 prisoners murdered in reprisal for the killing of a leading Bolshevik from Guria). After Vasha was posthumously resurrected by the Soviets, Levan was re-touched out of the picture, replaced by a shield on the wall.

Chapter 9

Vazha

Nihilism was a force, never far away from young minds during its great flowering in late 19th century Russia - and Georgia. A kind of incendiary for revolutionary movements, if not culture in general. Under the influence of its ever-present grenade in the pocket – as carried by Joseph Conrad's anarchist in *The Secret Agent* (1907) - centuries of religious convention were stripped away, and the emerging new politically-aware self, spoken-to directly. The philosophy could grant meaning to almost any activity at all; and arrived wrapped seductively in the arms of earlier writers like Ivan Turgenev (in his 1862 novel *Fathers and Sons*), and Fyodor Dostoyevsky (1821-1880).

In Georgia, one writer sometimes accused of being a devotee in his early career, was Vazha Pshavela (1861-1915) – real name Luka Razikashvili – son of a priest in the mountainous Pshavi region of northern Georgia.

But from these very remote, revolutionary beginnings was born, some say, the most original or distinctively 'Georgian' of all the nation's poets and short-story writers. One who quickly moved on from any youthful nihilism during his Telavi schooling and early teaching position in Toneti village. Who like Dostoyevsky developed a rich, religious perspective full of meaning – in Vazha's case, with nature. One might even say, Georgia's answer to nihilism. Many claim that more than any other Georgian poet or writer, Pshavela captured the distinctive voice of a people whose ancestors and language developed under the shadows of a huge mountainscape.

His most well-known poems, *Host and Guest,* and *The Snake Eater,* would be made into films and broadcast plays in the 20th century; be translated into Russian by admirers such as the poet Osip Mandlestam, who described *Pshavela's* poetry as,

CHARACTER in Georgia

'A real hurricane of the word... bubbling with the concrete, palpable, everyday... he seems to rip the words with his teeth, using the temperament of Georgian phonetics, which is passionate enough as it is.'
(from *A Few Things About Georgian Art*)

His famous, almost shamanic *The Snake Eater* (1901) was translated into English by Donald Rayfield, and broadcast by the BBC's Radio 3 in the UK. In this long poem, the protagonist Mindia, eats snake flesh, becomes able to hear animals and plants speak to each other – and him, because

> *'everything God created*
> *had language...'*

Underlying Vazha's poetry lies a streak of hard-core, mountain determinism. One could say, very Caucasian, as it carries a distinctive, pagan or animist streak - in the same way a form of pre-Christian paganism still exists in Georgia's high mountain regions - Pshavi, Svaneti, Khevsureti, Tusheti – and neighbouring Chechnya. Vazha tapped into something very original up there, confirmed by his decision to return to live and write in poverty back in his mountain village, after trying both St Petersburg and Tbilisi. He obviously found a greater meaning surrounded by nature's formative forces - even during the age of major social revolution. He then set out to convey what he'd found to his lowland, intellectual friends.

The opening of *Host and Guest* (1893) is all about the smallness of human ambition as set against the awe and majesty of the Greater Caucasus – a fact only too familiar to all the inhabitants of Pshavi.

> *Behind the buried gloom of night*
> *icy, pale to the eye*
> *Chechnya is a bare, rocky throne.*
> *In a gorge below the river roars*
> *its seething, inward wrath.*
> *The mountains bend down*
> *wash hands and faces in the spray,*
> *the souls of dead men*
> *living on their flanks...*

CHAPTER 9

...in the distance appears a Chechen village
perched like an eagle's nest
and as beautiful to observe
as a woman's breast.

The difference between his poems and say Shelley's or Byron's, who looked up at 'an Alp' then rhapsodised – is that Pshavela lived just about all his life among them. Although also stemming from a Romantic source, they're lined with the gritty reality of avalanches and flash floods. In so many of his poems, he speaks to mountains like consulting relatives. He asks them direct questions, queries their decisions, listens to their private arguments (as between a river and its stones in *The Rock and the River*), as if addressing a far more significant authority than the Tsarist administrators and Georgian nobility, against whom he rebelled during the day.

So what were the foundations of this far-seeing talent in Georgia's high Caucasus? The man who never seemed inclined to compromise, neither in literature or daily life – who is undergoing a revival today due to his powerful attraction to natural law. He even wrote short stories about an epidemic, *The Cholera Village,* and anti-smoking, *Pipe in the Dock.*

While growing up his child's eyes were surrounded by snowy peaks, deep forests, ravines, wild rivers and gorges in his home village of Chargali, set at 1200 metres, up in Pshavi - about a two-hour drive today, north from Tbilisi. He grew up in a three-room house (today a museum), its walls apparently so cracked that the wind could whistle through. He and his three brothers had a happyish family life, enriched by constant story-telling by their pastor father, Pavle. Most of the stories were biblical, but also mixed-in with Georgian folk stories and myths - possibly why Vazha employed Pshavi dialect in some poems. Vazha was particularly struck by dramas like David and Goliath and Samson. Indeed when Pavle noticed his sons' inclination towards literature, he encouraged them, even tried writing himself - creating his own memoirs; possibly the only father of eminent Georgian writers to do so.

Story-making was thus primed into Vazha's blood from an early age. Although his father couldn't afford university fees and had to work the fields like everyone else, he encouraged his sons to write. They attended schools in Tbilisi and two of the brothers managed to attend free courses in St Petersburg.

All four brothers exhibited the same independence of spirit and devil-may-care attitude. They loved to taunt their father with questions like - how could he be so sure God existed? To which he replied, how could they be sure he didn't? Adding, wasn't it them he just witnessed crying out 'God save us' when lightning bolts stabbed the ground as they scythed the mountainside grass?

Bachana, Vazha's younger brother - who would also become a talented poet - broke local tradition by marrying the girl who'd been his intimate friend. This is a centuries-old custom of the Pshavs and Khevsurs which allowed young men to have an official girl-friend pre-marriage. They were even allowed to sleep together, although apparently without the erotic element. However they were not supposed to marry - possibly echoing the wisdom of that much-heard contemporary phrase – 'Wish I'd married my second wife/husband first.' But Bachana followed his heart, went against tradition. His other brother, Tedo, also followed a literary calling, to become an outstanding children's writer - until killed in a village brawl.

Vazha himself opted for the career of school teacher - along with his two other brothers Bachana and Tedo. It could be they were the first ever qualified teachers from Pshavi. His initial positions were in the villages of Ertso (in Tianeti), and Toneti (near Betania, by Tbilisi). But by then his revolutionary instincts were finding voice. The local authorities, along with nobility and clergy, started receiving letters from parents complaining their children were receiving a 'nihilist education,' and being taught to resist the Empire.

In spite of many reprimands Vazha never baulked in this mission, seeing himself as the one to provide remote villages with a full and real education that included information about the *Narodnik* (people's revolution) movement, local injustice and its alternatives. It should be remembered that until the Soviet industrialisation and relocations, nearly half of Georgia's population lived in the mountainous regions (which is why so many abandoned stone villages are seen today). His teaching methods would involve many 'innovative' techniques – both in and out of the classroom.

CHAPTER 9

Once for instance, to focus attention on the fact a local priest was systematically fleecing his congregation, Vazha drew a target on the church wall, then began shooting at it. When asked why, he declared the priest - brother-in-law of the village leader – was corrupt, and the church itself asked for the bullets. On another occasion he instructed his students to bring a picture of the Russian Emperor to class, then systematically tear it up into as many physical pieces as possible. A kind of classroom performance art.

Not surprisingly the complaints increased, including some never-proved accusations of physical fights with members of the Toneti anti-education fraction. Finally inspectors were sent from Tbilisi to deal with them - and him.

Around this time comes a story of a government inspector called Darsky, who Vazha refused, point-blank, to allow into his classroom.

'Conduct your inspection from here,' he said pointing to a chair outside in the corridor

The frustrated official then, by chance, heard that Vazha's father Pavle, was visiting that same village. Darsky appealed to Pavle, and Vazha finally allowed Darsky into the class. Once facing the children, the inspector promptly drew a letter in the air and asked them to tell him which it was. Of course, nobody could.

So to illustrate the inherent double-standard of the authorities, Vazha quickly drew another pattern in the air and asked Darsky the same question. The embarrassed official had no idea either. This became the lesson of the day – on authoritarianism.

Most of Vazha's poems are set in remote mountain valleys, often illustrating the sense of honour between enemies – which always existed in the high Caucasus, until, some say, the Soviet regime. *Aluda Ketelauri,* opens in Shatili (in neighbouring Khevsureti), with a gun-fight between a Georgian and a Chechen (*Qisti*), who engage in conversation while re-loading their muskets, trying to kill each other. It might also be mentioned that in spite of their historic enmity, the Georgians, deep down, often supported their Chechen brothers over the larger invaders (like the Russians). When Stalin deported the entire population of Chechnya to Central Asia and the Khevsurs were given their mountain homes, the Khevsurs kept their belongings ready for the Chechen's eventual return in 1956-58. Even gave them livestock and tools, to re-start their former lives.

Seems that Vazha was trying to explain this intricate system of pride and respect that involved attack, even killing, but without slaughtering or removing entire populations. How to them, maintaining a complex sense of individual pride was more important than gaining absolutist dominance - as found in most lowland wars. Key to this was the sense of hospitality, explored in depth in *Host and Guest*, where,

> *'as a guest in another's house*
> *he can't launch the fight he wished.'*

However it can't be denied, most of his epic poems end tragically, with plenty of gore and blood-feuding. Dramas all the time haunted by the lonely, savage eye of a mountain Romantic.

After four years of rebellion in classrooms, Vazha eventually gave up teaching and became a professional writer - then a rarity in Georgia. He did occasionally augment his income with tutoring, as with the son of Prince Amilakhvari. But this didn't last. The boy was lazy and Vazha - who hated indolence - lost his patience and finally hit him over the head. The enraged princelet then returned with a shotgun - and employment was quickly terminated.

Now already married, Vazha returned to his home village. But even there the conflicts with authorities continued.

The calls for revolution, and Georgia's growing desire to leave the Empire, was thick in the air down in Georgia's towns and cities. On hearing about the developing revolution in Russia (failing in 1905-07), Vazha saw the chance for his country to finally gain its independence.

To bring the message back up into the mountains, he cajoled a local priest to make a tour of the remoter villages holding a cross, declaring the time for change had come; that villagers must now swear allegiance to 'the Revolution' as well as God. The priest, though terrified of Siberia (where he might be sent for such preaching), obeyed - because he feared Vazha's threatened whipping even more. Vazha had lost one of his eyelids earlier in life, giving his eyes a staring, tiger-like quality. This powerful double-act - trembling voiced priest and wild-eyed poet - gained many converts, and grateful presents. Apparently when Vazha

CHAPTER 9

returned home he regularly presented his wife with collections of trinkets – mostly liberated from the uniforms of village officials or devotees of the Empire.

It might be worth mentioning here, the description of Vazha by one of his brother's neighbours from his speech at Vazha's death. Vakhtang Kotetishvili – scientist and famous folklorist (shot in 1937), remembers Vazha walking up Vera Rise to his brother's flat.

'Vazha was not handsome, but there was something almost prehistoric in his black chockha, wide shoulders and determined step. He didn't walk, rather he moved like a heraldic beast. His pseudonym, Vazha Pshavela, summed him up perfectly. In those two words can be felt the force of the whole earth. One without horizon.'

Meanwhile his rebelliousness extended to other professions too. One of Vazha's friends from the highlands – Oziashvili - joined the local police. They would have long arguments over the nature of justice and enforcement. Vazha's wife would then receive more trinkets – Oziashvili's epaulettes and medals.

As a professional poet Vazha maintained an unusually strict defiance of the authorities and its officers. He never asked anything from the government. This even extended to not seeking assistance for his son Levan's, university education – which he would always regret. The same intransigence also applied to his daughter, Tamar's, studies.

But it was from his mountains, the ever-present icy peaks lurking behind the Chargali clouds, that Vazha imbibed his strength. Below is the full translation of one of his prose pieces - a new style of writing, suggested to him by one of his admirers, Ilia Chavchavadze, and penned in 1895.

The High Mountains

They were standing and waiting. Waiting outside time like the limitlessness of a sea. Their thoughts hid behind stone faces that said nothing, save that enmity itself awaits with them. That a fire boils in their summits, craving escape. But they have no voice. They stand and wait.

CHARACTER in Georgia

*Mountains, for whom do you wait? A lover perhaps — not seen
for an age? Or a child, brother or mother, so distant you have to
bend a rocky ear to the sky — then hear no answer? How can
you stand so motionless in this water that is the past, present
and future? Is your waiting really as old as the sea, as great as
limitless God?*

*Do you wait for a time when every flower, insect and breeze will
sleep, allow your huge exhalation, release your hidden cry of
stone? Are you like those men never admitting the rocks of
sadness clamped to their breasts?*

*Mountains, why don't you sing? Why should I die without
hearing this sweet sound? Why not laugh? Or just a tiny smile
for your friends? Why a slave to this granite of time, with all
life locked in your cliffs? Sometimes I think you only pretend, that
a happiness hides in your precipices. Does not just one small
candle light in your flanks when the eagle circles your summits,
rests a wing on your shoulder? How exquisite you are together!
He who you formed leans a head on your own. How handsome,
how obstinate he is! He is your messenger from God, for it is
he who informs God on you. Surely with him on your skin dreams
flow through your rocky mind. Of course they do! See all those
bright flowers nodding gently on your slopes — these are your
hopes.*

*But why then cover yourselves with mists? Perhaps you must hide
as you think. When you decide to deliver grass to us on your skin,
to drop down a cold stream, an avalanche, a prancing stag.
Sometimes I think you might lie, my friends. Am I right? And to
whom do you lie?*

*They are standing and waiting. Rain beats on their heads,
thunder plays in their eyes, lightning burns at their fringes and
their hearts. Does it matter if avalanches fall, if they bring down
skulls and stones? Flee all you who fear life under these heights
of sky. Go hide quietly down in the valley. Now it snows. The*

CHAPTER 9

mountains are covered with ice and cold. The stones are drunken
faces stuck to the slopes, covered in their shroud. They play
dead, they cry 'Bury us!' as we wait to be buried by them.

They are standing and waiting. I can feel a heartache under
those faces; a longing that never dies, that cannot die. For
whom, for what do they wait? Perhaps it is something invisible
to us . . . A possession that when they have it will simply demand
more and more. Could their wait be insatiability itself? Yes
surely that is it: insatiability is all they really are.

(Translated by P. NASMYTH & N. ANDRONIKASHVILI. From
the book *Georgia, in the Mountains of Poetry* by Peter Nasmyth)

As for this insatiability back down on earth, Gendarmerie records
of the turbulent 1905 Revolution period, mark Vazha down as a main
instigator up in Pshavi. Documents also blame him for helping his friend
Oziashvili be appointed as head of local police – a brilliant piece of
subversion.

As part of the official fight-back, around this time Vazha was
accused of by-passing the village's land ownership laws, by farming a
plot of unused land adjacent to his own (a common practice, even now).

When a squad of twelve soldiers came to reclaim the land, Vazha
found himself outnumbered and powerless to use his usual technique
of land retention - firing over intruders' heads (he was a renowned
marksman). They arrested him, tied his hands and escorted him to the
police station. But on arrival his friend Oziashvili promptly released the
poet.

However the shame of being marched off with hands-tied left
Vazha overwhelmed by a Pshavian sense of dishonour. But as chance
would have it, on the way home from jail he ran into two of the arresting
soldiers. He immediately accosted them and managed to wrestle away
one of their shotguns – which he took home as recompense.

Of course, disarming a police-officer, then stealing his weapon,
was a serious offence. Fortunately in the mountains then, such matters
could still be settled within their more traditional system of justice.
According to custom, Vazha was then politely asked to return the gun.

CHARACTER in Georgia

At the same time, and in the same tone, he was informed that if not, he would be promptly sent to Siberia.

Realising he'd no choice, Vazha returned the weapon. But to restore his sense of dignity, he then asked the soldier to kneel down before him and beg forgiveness for binding his hands.

After this curious but very effective ritual, the whole incident was considered closed. Indeed, after his death the disputed piece of land was renamed *Vazha Tskaro* (Vazha's spring), and can be visited today, close to the house museum.

As mentioned before, Vazha worked briefly for Ilia Chavchavadze's publication, *Iveria*. But his relationship with the paper lasted over 15 years. Chavchavadze recognised his remarkable talent and published everything he submitted, paying well. Once a historian and a journalist, Grigol Kipshidze, suggested a fundraising drive so Vazha could complete his education in Germany. But Ilia firmly rejected the idea, saying the poet would probably be seduced away into the ether of Germanic philosophy and give up poetry altogether. He insisted, wisely, Vazha's talent was perfectly located where it was. That any financial backing should be made to assist his life in Georgia.

But not every publication in Georgia liked Vazha's wild, tragic, animistic poetry, and he would receive many publication rejections.

One possible reason for his frequent failures may have been his well-known complaint about *Iveria's* decision to support the Georgian students in St Petersburg, by sending money for their studies. When asked to contribute he refused. He said the students should simply work harder and support themselves - as he'd done in St Petersburg. That if there was a will to study, they'd find a way. Furthermore that minor hardship would aid their concentration – in a similar way that Dostoyevsky's gambling and dire financial straits pressurised him to finish his stories.

He even wrote a public letter expressing as much, published in *Iveria*. In it he noted that when there was no oil for his lamp, he simply moved nearer to the fire to read and write. That he could compose poetry even while ploughing - simply stop briefly, scribble down words on the piece of paper always kept in his pocket.

The public didn't take to his letter; accusing him of being tight-fisted, unsympathetic.

CHAPTER 9

Some of the literary elite also criticised Vazha - claiming he merely 'lifted' traditional folk tales, and transcribed them into verse. That he wantonly borrowed plots and names, then used vague, disguising titles like *An Old Folk Story,* or *Ancient Legend.* But in truth much of this was done for the censor, concealing the fact that his stories often reported on actual contemporary events, which he prised into the old plots, to then slide past the suspicious eyes of the Empire.

But none of the criticism seemed to faze him. Like a kind of Snake Eater himself, the authority behind his voice always seemed bigger, like the mountains themselves. That he'd imbibed the visionary elixir of the high Caucasus, heard the voices of nature, given them a form of voice.

One of the elite resisting Vazha's work was the then famous Akaki Tsereteli. In the same way that Akaki's poetry had first been criticised as 'too sweet,' so he accused Vazha's as being too common, vernacular, abusing the lyricism of high Georgian ('I don't like your language, man from Pshavi...' he was rumoured to have said). He once even wrote a poem of his own, pastiching Vazha's occasional use of Pshavi dialect. Also he leant on editors not to publish Vazha's work - like Anastasia Tumanishvili, editor of *Kvali* a fashionable weekly. When Vazha learnt this, he wrote an open letter demanding that Akaki be removed from the *Kvali* Board.

A prickly relationship ensued, and the public were deeply curious to see if Vazha would be magnanimous enough to attend Akaki's 50th birthday, jubilee celebrations in 1908 (see poster at chapter end).

He did. Possibly as part of that Pshavian sense of respect for one's enemy - an important element of their (and Georgia's) hospitality tradition.

And the same might also be true of Akaki, who once publicly praised Vazha for confronting a visiting Cossack officer, Nikolai Ashinov, in the *Droeba* office. Ashinov had published an article declaring Russia should add Abyssinia to its Empire, in the same way it conquered, then added Siberia. *Droeba* had ridiculed the idea, so the Cossack arrived in full uniform, bristling with medals, demanding an apology. When none arrived, he threatened the editor, Sergei Meskhi, at which point the young Vazha Pshavela stepped up, grabbed the officer by the collar and physically threw him and his medals out of the building.

Vazha may have gained such skills during his teacher-training period in Gori, where he also studied boxing. Along with his elder, lawyer-brother Giorgi, Vazha entered local competitions between the Upper and Lower town. The Upper, known to be stronger, meant that Vazha preferred adding his talent to the Lower team.

And we might add a word here about Georgia's famous urban boxing tradition – if only because today we regularly see Georgians winning Olympic medals in Wrestling and proving themselves on the rugby pitch.

The sport had a name *'kviri,'* or *'saldastri,'* and started in Tbilisi as an organised, mass street-fighting competition. A kind of urban Martial Arts tradition. Usually around Lent and Easter, the city would gather together a number of opposing groups, according to districts – to then follow a pre-set fighting schedule. The first round would be fist boxing; one-handed, then two handed. The second, stone and stick boxing. Participants were divided into age-groups, beginning with small boys around the age of 10 – up to the seniors of 40 and upwards.

The winners were simply the group that pushed the invading neighbours back into their own territory. For instance, the Upper Town team, (above Abanoturbani) would try to push the Lower Town back behind the Garetubani (outside the city wall) border. Rather like a game of ball-less rugby inserted into heavily built-up, urban environment.

It could be very bloody. In 1851, 300 fighters were wounded and five died. The Russian authorities eventually made it illegal. So the tradition migrated to provincial towns like Gori, which already had its own strong wrestling and boxing tradition, that continued to be patronised by the nobility. A fact illustrated by the verse from a Prince Grigol Orbeliani's poem,

Look at me in Ortachala Gardens
Look at me feasting and joking
Look at me toasting
Look at me fighting with my fists
Then you know
Who I really am.

CHAPTER 9

As for Vazha, he also frequently teased his brother Giorgi, saying he wished his hunting was as good as his talking - accusing him of oiling and polishing his rifle, instead of using it. He declared him a *Tartarin of Tarascon*, after Alphonse Daudet's 1872 novel that satirised French arm-chair hunters. Giorgi defended his shooting prowess by mimicking the French nobility (and winding up his brother), claiming he rarely saw a stag worthy of soiling his rifle by firing at it. 'They don't have enough antlers anymore.'

But the person Vazha needed and cared for more than any other, was his wife. Tragically his first wife Keke had died early, leaving him a widower for two years, during which time, on top of everything else, he had to cook and prepare preserves for the hard, mountain winters. He kept his emotions to himself as was the tradition for high mountain men. Eventually he re-married a divorcee called Tamar. Initially they lived 'in sin' without a church wedding - in full-keeping with his rebellious nature.

Happily ensconced with his new wife, Vazha left his native Chargali only reluctantly. These would be his business trips to Tbilisi – when he'd gather his famous white horse Nikora, pack his saddle-bag with poems, then ride down the Aragvi river to make the rounds to various publishing houses. Once he'd collected enough royalties and new publishing deals, he'd return. But he often lost out – possessing the poet's ability to forget where his work had been published; sometimes *if* it had been published.

In town he'd always stay in Tbilisi at his younger brother Sandro's house in upper Vera (9 Khorava St), who always kept a room ready for him. There he'd work freely, blessedly released from the hard labour of his Pshavi fields. Very often it would be Sandro who'd first read his work.

A good way to end this account of this remarkable Georgian poet – the hardest of all to translate into English - is with a report from the memoirs of Sandro Shanshashvili, a popular poet and playwright - later close collaborator with Sandro Akhmeteli (1886-1937) in the Rustaveli Theatre. Shortly after the failed first Russian Revolution of 1905-7, Vazha had asked for a secret meeting in a Tbilisi tavern – saying he'd a carefully worked-out plan to present. Could Sandro find ten trustworthy men in Kakheti ready to sacrifice their lives for Georgia?

CHARACTER in Georgia

His idea was to identify 5,000 such heroes from around the country, then launch a surprise attack in Tbilisi and drive out the Russians.

Although deadly serious, with so many Revolutionaries already shot, arrested or exiled from the 1905 revolt, it quickly proved a non-starter. However ten years later, at the start of WWI, Vazha was convinced (along with others, like Akaki Tsereteli), the time had come again to free Georgia.

And freedom, albeit brief, would indeed come in 1918, but not until after Vazha's death in 1915.

Sandro, Vazha's youngest brother, recalled the day they discussed the Great War (1914-18) over an open map of Europe. Vazha made what seemed then, unbelievable claims about the end of the Austro-Hungarian and German Empires - even left notes on the map margins to that effect. Years later Sandro rediscovered the map and was astonished to see how accurate Vazha's predictions had been - like the shamanic figure this exceptional Georgian poet has since proved to be.

ANSWER TO THE HEART

I mix my sorrow and bile
with tears
use it for ink
tinted with vinegar
dripped in honey

As sweet for some
as sour for others
But it's not my fault
the nightingale
sings as loudly
on a thorn
as on a rose

Chapter 10

Wine, Tbilisi Life, City Planning

All Georgians love wine, so they say. So we better talk about it.

The Russian nationalist Vasily Velichko predicted that drinking would be the downfall of the Georgian nation. In terms of litres alone, he may have had a point. But as an outsider he failed to understand the ancient and very special relationship Georgians have with their national drink.

Nobles for instance, had a long history of making regular visits to each other's wine cellars, spending hours, if not days, tasting the wine direct from the *kvevri* (large, buried fomenting pots made our of clay). The process was aided by a traditional receptacle called an *azarpesha* – a long-handled silver drinking cup. At the end of a successful tasting, the visiting nobleman would often be given an *azarpesha*, some even adorned with precious stones - as a souvenir of this long-standing and important ritual. All part of that other no-less important ritual - friendship.

But like most traditions, this would develop over the centuries – especially with the introduction to Georgia of the drinking glass. Between the 13th and 19th centuries they were rarely used, although the 12th century chivalric epic *Amiran-Darejaniani* refers to drinking from glasses (see later this chapter). Horns of all kinds and sizes were the receptacles of choice. Families would often silver the lips of large horns as proof that an ancestor had drained it in one noble gulp. By the time of King Erekle II's reign (1744-1798) glasses had already made appearances on Georgian tables, but were generally regarded as inferior and too small. So the horn continued to dominate, especially at the grander feasts.

And these lavish, well lubricated *supras* were quite common at all levels of society. Indeed some say they played a crucial role in the nation's very survival, given its history of constant invasion and subjugation. This links back to the mountain tradition of welcoming your enemy into your house (see previous chapter), coupled with alcohol which served as a temporary equaliser.

When Russians arrived in Georgia at the start of the 19th century, glasses came with them – but were still rarely used for toasts, being too small. If used at all, several glasses would be placed upside-down in front of a diner, usually four, indicating the minimum number the person should drink. But still, at the climax of any feast, the horn would be produced. Some could hold over a litre.

Jean Chardin (1643-1713), a French protestant who moved to England, and was knighted by King Charles II in 1681, wrote up his travels to Georgia in a series of grand volumes *VOYAGES de Mr, le chevalier Chardin en Perse et autres Lieux.* In one episode he describes a banquet given by the then King of Kartli, Vakhtang V (1658-1675) in honour of his foreign guests. While Chardin it has to be said, includes plenty of unflattering descriptions of poverty across Georgia, on arrival at the banquet, his tone changes. Implication being, that even the misery of poverty could be overcome at a Georgian feast – where members of every level of society were present.

Chardin says the tables were laid out on a raised terrace, demarked by railings, with a huge tent stretched out overhead. Everything was beautifully presented, festooned with colourful cloth, mostly silk. It must have been late spring or early summer, because although warm, braziers (portable charcoal stoves) were laid out at regular intervals for the party's continuation into the evening – at a time when they were often used to heat homes (fireplaces were then rare and considered a luxury).

The King sat on a dais under a canopy, his sons and brothers on one side, the clergy on the other. Chardin and the guests were seated next to the latter. He noted that one of the local Princes had recently married, suggesting this could have explained the event's extravagance – he estimated at least 200 guests. A lot, even for a royal banquet.

Chardin was impressed how efficiently and silently the tables were attended. He went into some detail on the food and drinking customs. How initially guests only sipped their wine as they ate. Interestingly, he never mentions any toasting – at least what we think of as toasting today. This might seem bizarre, as conventional wisdom holds that Georgians need to deliver a toast before drinking.

CHARACTER in Georgia

At the time of Chardin's visit, the country was under heavy Persian influence. Because of this, starters were mostly rice, plain white or seasoned with cinnamon or pomegranate. The tables were covered by a wide variety of breads - from the paper thin, to thick and sweetened. This was followed by *kupati* – a chopped, spicy pork or roasted mutton, then *mtsvadi* – traditional Georgian *shish-kebab* or *shashlik* made with pork, beef or veal. Only after this course did the diners begin to drink in earnest. The author goes into some detail describing the separate table covered in drinking vessels, horns, goblets and cups. Because this was a royal banquet, all were either gilded, or even solid gold or silver. He counted eight identical cups which were then filled and handed to four people on either side of the King. These individuals then stood up and delivered their 'speeches of praise.' Not toasts in the modern sense, since the phrase's meaning in Georgian refers to clergy giving blessings.

Gradually the sizes of the arriving vessels grew in size, inevitably leading to increased drinking. The horns, chalices and other vessels were passed around the table in some sort or order, accompanied by the word *alaverdi* – borrowed from the Persian and meaning 'Allah be praised.' It subsequently came to mean 'passing the cup to you' in Georgian.

While the event carried plenty of Persian influence, rising to one's feet and drinking belongs to Georgia. Likewise he noticed the clergy received slightly different food, fish and vegetables, possibly related to their fasting. But when the foreign guests asked for the same, they were politely declined.

Chardin noted that one of the central figures at all feasts was the wine-bearer or pourer – known as *merikipe*. Incidentally Stalin was a particularly talented *merikipe*, staying sober and remembering everyone's conversations.

As the drinking increased, voices were raised, but Chardin stressed that the order and decorum was never broken. He also mentioned that the King ordered the foreign guests not be given the larger drinking vessels – guessing probably rightly, they lacked the same drinking talents as Georgians.

Possibly also why Chardin himself was able to give such a detailed account.

Though it may surprise some, Georgians do have a remarkable ability to organise – especially when it comes to feasts. Possibly because such banquets played an important role in the nation's survival – or the elaborate technique of making your enemy your friend. Chardin also mentions that a group of musicians sat somewhere nearby, in this case under the terrace, so music would drift gently up from below, adding to the conversations.

The Frenchman was impressed by everything he saw, not only by the amount of high-quality food and wine, but the expensive cutlery and dinnerware used in their presentation. This too seemed to play a subtle but important role in any such event - along with the possibility of overnight stays for guests and their servants. At this particular banquet he left at around midnight, but noted the feast was still only gearing up for its climax.

Just about every traveller to Georgia makes references to wine in their writings. However Georgia's own historical annals seldom mention it - probably because it was so integral as to be uninteresting. The amount consumed must also have been impressive for visitors, even a little baffling. In his travelogue about the Caucasian campaign *A Journey to Arzrum during the Campaign of 1829,* Alexander Pushkin recounts the story of a Russian soldier who managed to drown himself in a *kvevri* pot (which can be two metres deep), no doubt believing that diving-in was the fastest way to drink.

In those days even a relatively modest dinner would be blessed by a priest, who after delivering a short prayer, would 'praise' the food and guests. It could well be that the transition to a formal toasting tradition evolved from this, when hosts gradually took over this 'feast praising' role, then elaborated it.

As for supra locations, initially Georgians liked to hold their feasts outdoors, preferring the leafy walls and sounds of nature to those of their own homes. The host would scout out a particularly beautiful or welcoming scene/view in the nearby countryside, then lay out a suitably grand picnic.

Supras could also take place at night; a full-moon becoming another favourite backdrop. Even today one often runs into signs of such impromptu picnic spots in the hills around Tbilisi, and included music and dancing. In the early days *the* place to go was the Ortachala Gardens, in the south of the city. But now, with the advent of the 4x4, the reach has been extended, but is still usually not far from cities and towns.

To begin with, the land around Ortachala belonged to the last king of Kartli and Kakheti, Giorgi XII. It then passed to Archbishop Dositheos Gudushauri. But with its growing popularity, an Armenian merchant named Tershmanov bought, then developed it as a place for outdoor entertainment and relaxation. Good descriptions of daily life across the Caucasus can be found in Arnold L. Zisserman's *Twenty-Five Years in the Caucasus, 1842-1867.*

During that period the gardens sloped graciously down to the river. Soon they would be dotted with cabaret-style restaurants with singing, dancing, zurna bands and organ-grinders which well outnumbered the few taverns. This made it less of a drinking location, more the place to find a personal cook to prepare favourite dishes, al fresco. The nobility grew to love Ortachala, especially at night when candles would be hung from trees, with musicians wandering among them – all part of Tbilisi's long-standing tradition as one of the finest rest and relaxation stops on the Silk Road. The place where caravans always spent longer than intended.

Of course in those days the Mtkvari wasn't restrained by concrete walls and still flowed slow and wide at its own speed. People would pick nick at the water's edge on both banks, often greeting each other across the water, even holding conversations. Between them the river would be dotted with rafts, or 'floating tables,' as singing diners floated past, lit by torches. Under the influence of the bounteous grape, these could belong to any social or ethnic group, and all mixing freely together. Often people would recognise each other's voices in the dark. In the heat of summer, diners were known to jump into the river, swim over to a passing raft to join the revelries of another party.

One such occasion happened to the poet and Prince, Grigol Orbeliani – popular for his use of urban folklore and idioms in his poems. While in mid-feast on the riverbank, he noticed someone toasting him from a passing raft. He raised his glass and toasted back - at which point the rafter jumped into the river, swam over to the poet's group holding a fistful of freshly cooked *mtsvadi*. He then gallantly presented it to the poet and swam back.

Certainly this too would have been facilitated by the never far-away gallons. Alexander Dumas said the wine in Tbilisi was always good, often with a hint of sheepskin from its containers. He remarked that very rarely did he encounter bad quality wine.

CHAPTER 10

That feature it seems, was reserved for the 20th century when the Soviet Union initiated mass production of wine in the Caucasus. A time perhaps well described by Akaki Tsereteli's joke about poor quality wine – 'starting out as white, but turning red from shame.'

Inherent to places like the Ortachala Gardens, was the haphazard urban planning in pre-Soviet Tbilisi, created as much by instinct as any formalised blueprint.

This is well illustrated in 1912 when the well-known writer Ekaterine Gabashvili (1851-1938) was celebrating her birthday. Among her many presents came something completely unexpected - a gilded certificate from the Mayor's Office, signed by the members of the City Council, including the Mayor and Governor General. The text congratulated her for her sterling contribution to the city's urban development.

Baffled – for she'd never involved herself in any civic construction, or with the city Council – she made inquiries. City employees explained she'd been instrumental in creating the new housing estate they called Nadzaladevi (literally 'by force') in the capital.

Initially it had been an illegal shanty town made by a number of poor people moving to Tbilisi in search of work. The houses were more like sheds, built from found materials then patched together on a desolate, unused piece of land on the city outskirts.

Since they'd no permission to build, the police were sent to investigate and quickly concluded the area should be cleared, before it turned into a slum.

Shortly afterwards the police returned, this time with military back-up – only to be met by sticks, stones, clubs of all kinds, from desperate locals trying to keep their homes. In the end the police made a retreat without shooting – at the time firing of bullets was only permitted in life-threatening situations - to consult on how to proceed.

It was around then that Ekaterine Gabashvili wrote her short story *The Mshieradze Family,* about a poor family moving to the city outskirts in search of work, then building their own higgledy-piggledy shed - *mshieri* means 'hungry.' It illustrated how, in spite of their very basic conditions, the family lived happily enough and their neighbours were kind and considerate. The story made it to print in a local newspaper.

Mid 19th century engraving of a Tbilisi feast or supra held outdoors, probably in Avlabari region. The musicians would have been found specially for the occasion, and later 'musicians shops' would appear where they could be hired on the spot.

CHARACTER in Georgia

When the police explained the local resistance to their attempted clearance to City Hall, the Council sat down to discuss how to go about a forced eviction. But before any decision was made, one young Councillor stood up, asked if he could read Ekaterine's story to the chamber.

When the young man finished, the Council were stunned to silence. After a brief discussion, they decided to forego the eviction. Instead they imposed a symbolic price for permission to build on the slopes of Mount Makhata – which today borders Didube, itself bordering Nadzaladevi.

Although the price of a building permit wasn't high in Tbilisi, these worker families were charged less than usual, allowing that part of the city to expand rapidly.

Thus Ekaterine Gabashvili did genuinely contribute to the city's urban development.

It might be mentioned that it wouldn't be long before the inhabitants or 'workers' of this region would be agitating to install a new political regime – the Social Democrats, who, when taken over by their Bolshevik faction, would authorise the complete destruction of a large residential city district – Rikhe - on the eastern bank of the Mtkvari.

As for the area around Mount Makhata, it stood there rather barren and sad, uninviting for settlement. Very different to across the river in Mtatsminda, which had been turned into a green, classically architectured zone with parks and boulevards.

Perhaps this is why, when gallows were needed, the authorities usually chose Mount Makhata – although hangings were rare in the 19th century - about one every 10 years (except during the last Russian-Turkish war of 1877-78).

The area fell even more out of favour shortly after 1879 when the notorious robber Tato Tsulukidze, was hanged there. Tsulukidze who was only 26 – saw himself as a romantic bandit in the Arsena tradition (see Chapter 2). But the military tribunal disagreed, deciding he and his gang were no more than self-serving criminals requiring a very public and permanent removal. Anton Purtseladze's popular play from shortly afterwards – *The Robbers*, is based on Tato Tsulukidze's gang. The text carries strong parallels with Friedrich Schiller's famous play of 1781 *The Robbers*, and served as further intellectual stimulation for subsequent revolutionary movements.

CHAPTER 10

Some also believe that Ilia Chavchavadze described that very hanging in his story *On the Gallows*. But there's a slight problem here. The story was written just prior to Tato's execution – though of course the writer's admirers claim that Ilia Chavchavadze possessed sufficient foresight to predict the outcome of Tato's arrest.

Another example of literature influencing public officials…?

Who knows.

But some phrases from Purtseladze's play, like the robbers' real names, entered common parlance – as being synonymous with crime. Because executions were so rare, each hanging is well remembered. Like the two, 20 years earlier, when the Tbilisi criminals Shubashev and Ismail, met similar ends in the same place, for an extraordinary, bungled crime.

They had decided to rob a Tbilisi jeweller called Jorjiev, and befriending his two sales assistants, invited them to a tavern intending to steal the workshop key. The assistants protested they didn't have it; that Jorjiev never trusted anyone with keys. So the robbers simply killed them then concocted the ridiculous idea of donning their clothes, returning to the shop assuming Jorjiev would simply open the door to these similar-looking people. But of course, the jeweller spotted the men had different faces, kept the door locked and they were soon arrested.

To balance out this story we might mention a slightly more pleasant end-of-life tale from around then - that of the famous Tbilisi Casanova, Bekalmashev. By then this retired Russian army officer was already well-greyed, but not it seems his romancing. According to legend he ended his days in the throes of ecstasy with one of his secret amours. But she became less secret when locals started coining the phrase about ending one's life using,

'the Bekalmashev method.'

To follow one tasteless anecdote with another, one might also mention a similar expression from that time. Two men in the Asian part of Tbilisi (like Kala), while watching women walking past, might be heard to remark;

'She's from our quarter.'

Which meant - a prostitute.

'Our quarter' was the nickname for the area around Meidani, behind the sulphur baths, known for its Azeri tea houses and brothels.

Eventually the local Sunni Muslims became fed up with the noise and frequent brawls around these ill-reputed houses. They complained and the City Council moved the trade to a less conspicuous street in the back of Ortachala. So business continued, but less obviously.

Interestingly there's no recorded history of prostitution in Tbilisi before the 19th century. Seems such ladies of the night first arrived along with the Russian troops during their southward expansion of the Empire. As the army also brought with it new military highways, roads, post-offices, horse-change stations, this inevitably led to taverns. Thus the oldest profession gradually spread itself across the country, tavern to tavern.

As for the women themselves, most were unfortunate young peasant girls, sold on by their landlords to merchants and inn-keepers.

Soon it wasn't only prostitution that was spreading across the country along the new roads - but ideas. The population became steadily more knowledgeable then vociferous in their desire for change. Revolution was in the air. And with it came new catchphrases and ever more seductive political theories. Some of their more prominent mouthpieces would turn to the new theatre buildings, which from the 1880s started to sprout in the larger cities and towns.

For instance, one evening in Kutaisi, when the new theatre happened to be full of gendarmes (political police), the actor Lado Meskhishvili suddenly broke out of his stage character and shouted down to the audience, 'Victory to the people!' five times - though twice would probably have been enough. Later the theatre would become named after him – no doubt for his Revolutionary heroism. For of course, 'the people' would achieve their victory, after the 1917 Revolution. Or so they were told from other political stages.

This became merely part of a long series of stage-delivered messaging. One of the first happened some years earlier at one of Alexander Tairov's (1885-1950) theatres when playing *The Homeland*, by Davit Eristavi (1847-1890) in Tbilisi. Premiered in 1882, this Georgian version of the French play *La Patrie* by Victorien Sardou, was probably initially performed in Russian. However Eristavi switched the drama's main confrontation between Holland and Spain, to Georgia and Persia. Furthermore it daringly featured a defiant Georgian royalist flag in the final scene – news of which even reached Moscow. More details of this are found in the next Chapter.

One young Tbilisi worker, Gigo Basilashvili, watching the play with friends, became so affected that on the way home, when encountering some Muslim water-carriers, he promptly attacked them. The young men were immediately arrested and found themselves facing serious charges - such spontaneous, aggressive acts were then rare in Tbilisi. In his memoirs Basilashvili said he pleaded with the police, explaining the performance had so overwhelmed his sense of reality, he believed the Muslims were Persian invaders. However, now fully recovered, he would accept any punishment for his terrible behaviour, even exile to Siberia. But he begged the police to please 'forgive the actors' for delivering such convincing performances.

The police let them go.

Wine, or possibly water delivery carts, in the 19th century

CHARACTER in Georgia

We might end this chapter on wine with a story from a 12th century, hand-written epic by Mose Khomeli *Amiran Darejaniani* – a heroic-deeds epic, telling tales of wandering, chivalrous knights travelling the world doing good. It depicts a famous knight, disguised in ordinary clothes, being invited by strangers to a *supra*.

'We ate,' said the knight, 'then the host stood up, filled his glass and said to me, 'May Almighty God glorify and give a long life to Sepedavle, the greatest knight to ever walk this earth!' He drank and sat down. Then he filled the same glass and passed it to me, saying, 'Now you praise Sepedavle!' But I answered. 'Sorry, I've come to fight Sepedavle, and until he defeats me, or I him, I will never praise him!'

Later the two knights met in the competition and the guest-knight defeated Sepedavle. But afterwards, as is the tradition, both sat down together at the banquet, toasted each other and continued the process Georgian feasts always hope will happen. That the enemies - usually the invader of Georgia and the invaded - drink enough wine together to become friends.

At least for a while.

ფერი-ფერსა

მადლი დმერთსა

ღვინოვ კახურო, ვარ შენი მსმელი,
გინდ თეთრი იყოს, გინდა წითელი,

სუფრასა ვზივარ, შენს ნახვას ველი,
უშენოდ არ ვარგა, ოქროს საჭმელი.

Chapter 11

The Theatre

Some have said Georgians are born with the instinct for drama running through their veins. So no surprise then, even before the new profession of actor arrived in the country in the 1880s, theatres had been sprouting up, first in Tbilisi, then just about everywhere. As if a new religious cult had been seeded and fertilised, to then flower wildly across the country.

Thus when Georgia's first-ever, full-time dramatic-arts company was created in Tbilisi, it landed into a culture already fully embracing it. All the faces on either side of the stage arch were enthusiastic, eager to work on this new art of self-presentation. And suitably, the first set of actors were all angelic looking. Every word they pronounced on stage carried the tone of collective purpose and artistic hope. A kind of intellectual miracle, heightened by the fomenting national independence and Revolutionary ideas swirling around the general population.

But good theatre, of course, depends on there being good plays. Fortunately, plenty were finding their way over from Europe into Georgia. They ranged from classic Shakespearian tragedies, (the best translated by Ivane Machabeli), to fluffy, home-grown comedies – and just about everything in between. Initially the spectacle itself proved as powerful as the messages in the plays. Probably the most popular – at least from the 1880s up until 1917 - was *Samshoblo* ('The Homeland'), by David Eristavi, a well-known lawyer from Tbilisi. Staged literally hundreds of times, and to rapturous receptions, the action amounted to a heavily Georgianized version of *La Patrie!* (1879) by the French playwright Victorien Sardou. As previously mentioned, the play included the dramatic entrance of the Georgian royal flag. The play was so successful that Russian nationalist critics in Tbilisi and later Moscow, tried to trash it. *Moskovskie Vedomosti* declared the flag should stay where it was displayed – in the circus (due to the absence of theatres, many early productions took place in circus buildings). Ilia Chavchavadze, although not much of a theatre fan, wrote a stiff, and much praised riposte in his essay - *Answer to Kadkov* (Kadkov was the editor of *Moskovskie Vedomosti)*.

'For two thousand years Georgians have carried the Georgian flag and name with honour, poured their own blood into it, then passed the flag over to Russia ready for use, when they needed it. During our joint battles Georgian blood flowed and blended with Russian. We carried this flag reverently and for so long, against seas of Tartars and Muslims. Like Jesus's cross we protected it, then we planted it back on Caucasian soil. It is the same flag that today Georgians follow alongside Russia's... and now someone in Moscow calls it a circus flag? Even a barbarian would be ashamed of that word...'

The actors in the company were mostly young, inexperienced, but with that same natural-born talent we still see in modern Georgian drama. For theatre opened up an entirely new avenue for communication and self-display. Also it carried that important, slight distance from reality - the proverbial proscenium arch well set between the dangerous world of the stalls. A once-removed vista on human life and its politics, offering the nation a more objective view on itself. To the adoring audiences, the possibilities of this new art seemed limitless.

It wasn't long before almost every street had its own mini-theatre – in the same way that today many yards carry football goals, or basketball hoops. Children would play-act, just as they now kick and throw balls.

It may not be too big an exaggeration to say, much of this major new fashion spawned out of a single professional troupe. The Georgian Theatre Company was founded just after the Russo-Turkish war (1877-78) when urban restrictions were relaxed and the newspaper *Droeba* began to devotedly cover all performances. The same company exists today –renamed The Rustaveli Theatre Company.

But its reach soon extended beyond Tbilisi. As an all-Georgian and all-Georgia troupe, its eyes were set for expansion, border to border, if not beyond.

Their first tour was something extraordinary for Georgia - again very in keeping with the local character. Indeed, the same enthusiasm is still felt in the gusto and sophistication of Georgia's modern audiences.

Bad performances are met with the banging seats from departing punters; good ones with rapturous cheering and clapping.

After the company's first professional performances in the Tbilisi spring of 1878, they launched an ambitious summer tour. The group travelled to Gori, Kutaisi, Poti and Batumi, accompanied by two large crates of props, then played the same cities again on the return leg, adding Borjomi and Akhaltsikhe. A smallish troupe of nine actors - five men and four women, though without their founder/Director, Giorgi Tumanishvili (1854-1920). A hugely demanding trip, but one that none of the participants, or any that witnessed it, would forget.

Maybe the words 'men' and 'women' aren't strictly accurate, as then people of this age were often called 'boys' and 'girls.' The oldest actor was 27, the others between 20 and 22. Their names - Vaso Abashidze, Asiko Tsagareli, Zaal Machabeli, Nodar Jorjadze, Kote Kipiani, Babo Korinteli, Masho Kipiani, Nato Gabunia and Mako Saparova, would become celebrated nationwide. The punishing schedule required resilience, especially from the actresses, who engaged in a radically new role for Georgian women. Occasionally other actors joined along the way - like Kote Meskhi in Kutaisi.

The overall effect was to leave most audiences spell-bound and a lot of people dreaming of a new career pacing the wooden boards.

The company was well organised, even had a resident prompter - the journalist, Gigo Kipshidze – formerly Ilia Chavchavadze's right hand man at *Iveria*. He also served as a translator - fortunately a good one - as the others rarely did the texts any favours. They were also accompanied by an administrator, Adam Chubinashvili, and hairdresser/stylist, Davit Amirejibi. Indeed, with such a list of noble families, the troupe could have been re-named The Nobility.

But in spite of their origins, the troupe remained mostly penniless – though cheerful. For the tour widened their horizons in a way none could have dreamed.

First stop was Gori, home of the leading actresses, Nato Gabunia. It might even be said Gori was Georgian theatre's primary launchpad out into the wider world. For the arrival of the first-ever professional troupe generated such a feverish atmosphere, the platform at the railway station bulged with a crowd large enough to greet the Emperor. This was followed by the usual chaotic scenes of competing Georgian hospitality with actors invited to stay in homes across the town. However, needing some cohesion, they all ended up at the rich philanthropist, Zuriashvili's house. They had three comfortable rooms, separated for men and women, and stayed there for ten days.

More importantly, a not-too-bad space was found for their performances – the open air Rotonda, near the old bridge. In those days sufficiently large halls were rare – even for modest productions. Local amateur dramatics usually took place in restaurants or school assemblies.

As everyone knows, Georgian hospitality can be excessive; but it would still be hard to top the lavishness showered on those first professional actors. Some of the Gori playwrights, most now forgotten, like Aghalo Tutashvili, embarrassed everybody by their effusive, fawning admiration. Aghalo flatly refused to allow the actors to spend any money, inviting them to dinner after dinner. Since food and accommodation were free, all income from their sell-out performances went straight back to the production. And these young Gods and Goddesses from Georgia's future, should never be asked to *pay…*

Indeed, the entire town rallied round and supported the productions - sewing curtains, building sets, creating advertisements. The theatre generated a community spirit and delightful relief from the daily grind of life and its politics.

Even Niko Diasamidze, a notorious local landlord, known for his explosive temper and sarcasm, transformed into a sycophant hanging meekly around their accommodation, asking how he might possibly help.

So that's how it all began - in Gori. Not surprisingly, word spread rapidly and similar welcomes would greet their journey all the way across Georgia.

As for the actors themselves; apart from Kote Kipiani, none had even crossed the Surami mountains – the dividing line between West and East Georgia. They travelled, noses glued to the train windows, often still pestered by admirers who followed them onto the train, clinging desperately onto the coat-tails of the event. Furthermore genuine romance was in the air. The actors Vaso Abashidze and Mako Saparova were in love.

But even that was briefly forgotten when the train arrived at Kutaisi. The troupe was met at the station by a sea of flowers, waving arms and wildly cheering voices. Their fellow actor Kote Meskhi had arrived in advance, summoned a crowd of the town's students, noblemen, officers, merchants to welcome this new art-form to a city which considered itself the most modern in Georgia. Certainly Kutaisi was then affluent, possessing a substantial bourgeoisie and intellectual community.

Its best hotel on The Boulevard, the Iveria, gave over a whole floor to the troupe – maybe part explaining why the building later housed the famous Kharazov theatre.

Like in Gori, Kutaisi didn't have any proper venue for theatre performances. The best it could offer was a crude wooden Circus, with a tin roof that baked its audience in the summer – in spite of water being constantly being poured on it from barrels.

When the troupe announced its first show, the comedy *Pepo*, by Gabriel Sundukiants, (Armenia's foremost playwright, born in Tbilisi, who translated his Armenian-language plays into Georgian himself), crowds queued from early morning for tickets. Meanwhile the necessary and rapid upgrading of the Circus was overseen by Kote Kipiani, aided by an army of volunteers. The backdrop was painted, wallpaper and chandeliers donated from private homes.

Everywhere the company landed, they seemed to bring a small piece of enchantment with them. Many felt this was the European future, until then hidden from far-away Georgia, finally arriving. And it came represented by a cast of bright young Georgian faces.

Kutaisi was smitten. As soon as the curtain raised, the audience stood up in rapt attention, cramming into the Circus building, or listening eagerly from adjacent streets. An entirely new experience for the city.

Nor did the ensuing Imeretian hospitality disappoint the actors, for none had tasted East Georgian food before. Indeed one day a group of women arrived bearing nine identical blue shirts – hand-sewn with silver buttons and narrow white trim. The actors immediately donned them, which led to a new kind of performance – walking through the city. As soon as they were spotted the actresses' many admirers were soon competing to present ever more extravagant gifts – many that they treasured for the rest of their lives.

After Kutaisi lay Poti and Batumi on the Black Sea – two cities with grand new ambitions, thanks to the burgeoning oil business.

It must have been hard to say goodbye to Kutaisi, but the troupe prised themselves away – though not before Vaso Abashidze and Mako

CHAPTER 11

Saparova were married in Kutaisi's Bagrat cathedral. Thus they became Georgia's first ever theatre couple. The second would be Asiko Tsagareli and Nato Gabunia.

Leaving Kutaisi in the full summer heat, they regained their strength on the train and headed west to Poti. None of the company had ever seen the sea, and mistakenly celebrated the mouth of the river Rioni as the Black Sea. As for the city itself; another revelation. Small but well-designed in a grid system, with its zones neatly defined – very unlike the winding, Asian streets of Tbilisi.

Poti had two good hotels: The Alain and Charcot, which duly housed the company. Their tour was hosted by Prince Jambakur Gurieli, a larger-than-life character who, with his wife Eleonora, feted the young actors and found a school-hall for their performances. As for the necessary gastronomical entertainment - a good match for Kutaisi, with four-course breakfasts; eight-course dinners, except on performance days. For the grand finale Prince Gurieli laid out a long *supra* table in the park, hosting a banquet that went on well into the night. But just as it seemed to be ending, Gurieli stood up and announced 'the champagne boats' had arrived. To the actor's astonishment the banquet then shifted itself onto rafts, to be floated out onto Lake Paliastomi accompanied by the sound of popping of corks.

Thus it could well be said, these actors became Georgia's first-ever true celebrities, in the modern sense. Before this tour they could walk unrecognised down any street in the country. Afterwards, they became living icons in every town they performed. Locals believed it their duty to shower them with gifts and admiration, almost as they would saints.

Thus a group of penniless travelling actors, ended up as a new kind of spiritual royalty in Georgia.

Next was Batumi, a city only just re-taken from Turkey. But due to its three centuries neglect under the Ottomans, it still remained inaccessible by rail. And with the roads unmarked and in terrible condition it was said only bandits knew the way between Guria and Ajara. So, a boat was required.

Only three maintained any regular service from Poti - *Babushka* (granny), *Dedushka* (grandpa) and *Rioni*. After Prince Gurieli's lavish banquet, the troupe boarded *Babushka* for Batumi.

CHARACTER in Georgia

Oskar Schmerling cartoon of a Georgian officer trying to charm a lady. 19th century Georgia

This soon-to-be, Georgia's third city, turned into another miraculous experience for the actors. Although smallish in population, it housed a large port, Russian administration and military settlement, along with several parks peopled by plenty of dashing Georgian officers. The population was a mix of Georgians, Russians and unusually, Europeans. Furthermore, it held a substantial population of Muslim Georgians who stayed on after Batumi was reunited back into Georgia. Above all perhaps, Batumi was a 'free port,' where cargoes and goods escaped taxation. Everything in the shops was considerably cheaper than the rest of Georgia, partly as a result of its frenetic, oil-industry growth.

One of the actors, Asiko Avksenti Tsagareli – author of Georgia's most popular comedy (even to this day), *Khanuma,* - wrote an account of visiting Batumi twenty years later, saying it felt as if Mtskheta - the small ancient Georgian capital – had suddenly turned into Tbilisi. He remembered how a bottle of French cognac cost just 1.5 roubles, while exactly the same bottle went for 9.5 in Tbilisi. The difference in prices was so striking, the whole troupe managed to refresh their entire wardrobe for years to come.

CHAPTER 11

Although Batumi was still recovering from its garrison town role, its Mayor, Colonel Bers and his Georgian wife were highly cultured. The couple provided many a grand breakfast for the actors. Furthermore the Mayor made sure that the head of Batumi Police, Durmishkhan Zhuruli, greeted the troupe personally when they first disembarked. His son Giorgi, then a student (later a prominent journalist and Georgian censor) watched the troupe arrive open-mouthed; especially at the actresses – then a radical new profession.

Shortly after their arrival the actor Vaso Abashidze had to suddenly return to Tbilisi due to his father's illness. His acting roles were quickly taken over by Gigo Kipshidze. This left the company needing a prompter. Many locals volunteered, and Giorgi was chosen. He then watched, not only the performances, but mountains of gifts being delivered to the actresses by the stream of admiring army officers. So he decided to do the same.

He ordered a large bouquet on his father's account and boldly presented them to Nato Gabunia. While it achieved a moment of mild embarrassment in the actress, it was the Batumi florists who experienced the full delight. Spotting the love-struck teenager, they charged his father 25 roubles – the Batumi equivalent of 17 bottles of French cognac - for the single bunch of flowers.

Then there was the problem of publicity. Batumi had no printing house, and the troupe had no posters left from Poti. So someone had the bright idea of teaching the city's Muslim water-bearers, to shout out the exact titles, locations and times of that evening's performance. Soon the company discovered that if the names of actresses were added, the audience numbers increased.

It wasn't long before the actresses were joking about which of their names would be shouted first, and how loud. Sometimes, spotting a water-bearer, they'd rush up, give him a coin and instructions on how to pronounce their name.

As for the audiences; demonstrations of admiration were often, if not usually OTT – especially from the Georgian officers. During the goodbyes at Kutaisi station, not wanting the actresses to physically leave, they'd jump onto the carriage roof; swing themselves down into the doors, then relentlessly flatter them all the way to the Rioni river estuary. Others followed the train on horseback, throwing flowers in through the train windows.

CHARACTER in Georgia

Not wanting to be outdone, in Poti Georgian officers took to boats, delivering final flower-tosses up at the departing hull of *Babushka*. It might be noted that due to the newness of the art-form, some actually believed the actresses were the same people they played – thus giving these romantic gestures a strangely fantastic element.

In Batumi the troupe also met the local nobility – including a number of Muslim Princes. They too were impressed by the new art-form. But rather than hosting the troupe at grand, wine-drinking feasts, they invited them to the city's splendid, mirrored tea-houses, treating them to fine spreads of coffee and sweets. Their most frequent question was about life in the eastern side of Georgia, a place they'd never seen.

One day an elderly, grey-bearded bey approached the male actors, most of whom wore fashionable city caps, saying;

The restaurant and dance hall in Mushtaidi Park, Tbilisi, late 19th century (since gone). Such buildings would also have been used for lessor theatre performances and events. Today the park (Tbilisi's oldest) still survives along with a similar styled wooden building, though in need of repair and restoration like so many of Georgia's elegant historic buildings

"You're all excellent young men, but pardon me if I say your hats look a bit like pigs' snouts."

With this he promptly presented them with a set of fezzes, proceeding to demonstrate how to gently touch the rim, as a greeting.

So exactly as in Kutaisi, the actors donned the fezzes and their blue-shirted costumes, then walked the Batumi streets, making the appropriate greetings.

Just another example how theatre can bridge seemingly impassable gaps between cultures, bring smiles to the faces of those who'd just emerged from a three-hundred year, very harsh occupation of their home city.

Chapter 12

Guria

That word 'Guria.' In Georgia often it carries a slightly reverential tone. Especially if you're a politician or socialist. Two heads of state and nearly all the founders of Georgia's Menshevik government, (1918-21) hail from this small region of around 100,000 (one out of Georgia's eleven), tucked away under the Lesser Caucasus mountains. It's been called the 'Nazareth of Socialism,' compared to Prussia in Germany; and there's an old joke - that Guria has only two real exports, mandarins and intrigue.

Regarding the latter: during Georgia's critical, early 20th century period, Guria gained a unique kind of independence, known as 'The Gurian Republic.' And there *is* something a touch reverential, even historic about it. The process of its creation began around 1902 and flowered 1905-06 when Guria actually renamed itself 'The Republic of Ploughmen and Sowers.' The local population managed to manufacture an entirely new form of communally structured government which took over the state and had a strong influence on the formation of Georgia's own independent Social Democratic (Menshevik) government (1918-21), which of course, ruled all of Georgia. There can be no doubt that the Gurian experiment - which established its own community councils and courts, libraries, fair distribution of labour, and women's suffrage – was used as an example, even template, for that far grander revolution up north; the one eventually harbouring dreams of world domination.

Is that an exaggeration? Well, Lenin himself referred to it many times, even intended writing a chapter on it (though eventually never did); and shortly before his death Leo Tolstoy declared in a letter to Ivane Makashidze, '...*what's happening in Guria is of immense importance. Although I'm aware the Gurians haven't heard of my existence, I nevertheless have a great desire to express to them the ideas and*

CHAPTER 12

sentiments they have awakened in me by their admirable movement.' (Quoted by Luigi Villari in his *Fire and Sword in the Caucasus*.)

Interestingly, 60 years earlier, a previous 'Gurian Revolt' (1841), may well have set up the blueprint for the second. On that occasion the peasants and nobility rose up as one against the Russian occupiers, taking control of the state for a few bold months, before being summarily crushed by soldiers of the Empire.

There are several reasons for this unusual independence of mind flowering out by the Black Sea. But all probably stem from one fundamental condition - poverty. Guria was then, not only the poorest region of Georgia, but probably the whole Russian Empire.

So, the initial 'reverential' word might well be followed by another, slightly less reverent – *pirali*, the term for a local bandit. Those two go hand in hand and had some strong bearing on the Social Democratic movement that swept through the region just after 1900. A blend of bandits and fervent idealists would help create what some have claimed the world's first, genuine Social Democratic state (the rival one in Queensland, Australia of 1899 lasted only a week). A government that would then lead to the creation of the first Social Democratic country - Georgia, between 1918 -21. A group of inspired Gurians effectively ran their own communal fiefdom for several years – until they too were stamped out of existence by Tsar Nicholas II's systematic clamp-down following the failed 1905 Revolution in Russia.

Before that period of historic Republicanism, most mentions of Guria conjured images of this specific brand of bandit. While there were robbers and highwaymen lurking in all of Georgia's forests, the *pirali* were different from their counterparts in Kakheti or Kartli (see Chapter 2), or probably anywhere in the world.

So, what exactly was a *pirali*? Certainly a bandit, but from the more idealistic branch of that tree. The difference was their willingness to fight other, less idealistic bandits and with as much ferocity as the unjust, social inequalities imposed by the Empire. This type of outlaw had a character that fit in with the slightly less showy and impulsive Gurian personality – as compared with the eastern Georgians.

Some will argue a bandit is always just a bandit, whether self-proclaimed 'honest' or not. That even Georgia's prototype Robin Hood, Arsena, was never more than just a glorified thief.

But in Guria they could be wrong.

One might even say that the practical beginnings of modern Socialism grew out of the mentality of this remote peasantry lurking under the Lesser Caucasus mountains. One setting its feet on the poor man's sense of fairness, blended with a code of chivalry – and a bit of intrigue. That it traversed all levels of society – from nobility, ploughmen and sowers, all the way down to bandits. This itself stood on a curious form of education derived less from schools - which were very ill-equipped in Guria – than priests. The dogged spreading of the Gospel induced a strong love of storytelling and a kind of home-grown literacy, unusual for such poverty-struck regions. Thus when the new Gospel according to Social Democracy arrived, it quickly spread on already fertile ground.

To investigate the germination of this *pirali* character, we might spend a moment focussing on the life of one particular *pirali* back in the 1880s. The story of Gogia Lomjaria, a young man of around 22, who rented out horses and transportation in Batumi.

At the time, Gurian life was particularly hard for all such working-class people – jobs were scarce, agriculture undeveloped and poverty endemic. This small state paid huge taxes to the Russian administration – up to 300,000 roubles a year (taken mostly from the peasantry) – who'd then spend less than 20,000 back on the region, and most of that on police and bureaucrats. But it should also be mentioned, Gurians and Georgians generally, still wanted a Russian military presence in their country - to protect against their historic enemy, the Turks. The memories of their Muslim occupation in the Russo-Turkish War of 1877-78 were all too fresh. They weren't anti-Russian, simply demanded a fairer system.

Due to poverty many Gurians had been leaving for nearby cities, like Poti and Batumi, seeking work. Their natural skills in woodworking had some application in the new construction and oil industries.

Gogia had recently married, so worked hard to earn money to begin a family. Part of his job involved driving or delivering other people's cows and horses. A harmless occupation, seemingly. But unfortunately, not everyone in that time of poverty possessed the same sense of integrity.

It's no secret that low-ranking nobility could also be thieves – while still flaunting their titles. Many, having lost their land, were now washed-up and penniless (as described in Chapter 1). It seems one such individual had secretly stolen a cow, then paid Gogia to deliver it to another village. But en-route the owner spotted it and Gogia was arrested as the thief. Following the long-established Gurian code of silence and non-betrayal, in court Gogia said nothing in his defence. At that time all informers were looked-down-on; could even be killed for snitching. Feeling himself built into this category, Gogia protected his 'noble' employer - wrongly. However once found guilty, he mentioned the fact of his innocence to the District Aide, explaining he was only offered the usual fee for cow delivery, so please could the punishment be lenient.

Unfortunately for Gogia Lomjaria again, the District Aide happened to be Prince Anton Nakashidze. The Lomjarias had been their family's serfs before the abolition of serfdom several decades earlier. But the mentality of the nobility had not been abolished.

In spite of Gogia's pleas, Nakashidze repeatedly threatened Lomjaria with exile in Siberia. The alternative - a large fine - would be almost as disastrous for a man as impoverished as Gogia. Gogia even tried reminding Nakashidze his family were once their serfs. It didn't work. He received a crippling fine. Then, so the story goes, Prince Anton's brother, Meliton Nakashidze – one of the dissolute Princes – began whispering in Gogia's ear.

"Can't you see my brother had it in for you? I'd say he deserves a bullet, don't you?"

Rumour had it he wanted his brother's job.

But who really knows.

Whether it was Meliton's encouragement or his own heart, Gogia then confronted Anton Nakashidze on his way to work, and raised his pistol.

According to some accounts, Gogia had previously decided to let the bullet determine if his action was justified or no. If it struck home, he'd be fully vindicated. If it missed or only grazed Nakashidze, then the Prince would be entitled to live on, and he receive the full punishment – Siberia at the very least.

He fired and the Prince dropped dead.

In that moment Gogia became a *pirali*.

His kind of story isn't so uncommon among most of the other outlaws in Guria. Very few were vicious thugs, most just poor peasants whose lives had been pitched cruelly against the unfair vagaries of the law; victims of an antiquated system that needed urgent reform. And Guria had plenty of forests in which to hide.

According to publications of the time, about 60 *pirali* roamed Guria in the 1880s. Inside their leafy hide-outs they'd meet, swap stories and get to know each other's lives and ideas. Gradually this camaraderie of oppression and long night-time discussions – became influenced by the new Social Democratic ideas. Soon the *pirali* began to see themselves as a new kind of non-law-abiding police force. The poor would never be touched, and they'd justify their robberies by following their own instinctive sense of right and wrong – like Gogia and his bullet. As they saw it, if the real law favoured injustice, then their own far fairer version, had every reason to replace it.

Some would say this arbitrary form of justice was too dependent on the integrity of the individual. But in Guria particularly, it connected to a long-established sense of pride in their personal character. One that exists to this day and still reaches deep into most inter-personal Georgian relationships. And this helped it work. Indeed that sense of a brotherhood forming in the forest, showed itself again in the late 20th century, where Georgian partisans in the Gali district of Abkhazia after the 1991-3 civil war, referred to themselves as 'The Forest Brothers.' Furthermore, when the Gurian Republic established itself during 1905, the same processes became central to the new peasants' or 'People's Courts.'

In the meantime, the *pirali* operated mostly as highwaymen, but of course, the discriminating kind. Their mission gathered a socialist edge, protecting the poor, not only from the injustices of the Empire's militia, but other bandits. There are several tales of merchants being waylaid by *pirali,* being asked only for a coat and some cash on behalf of someone else, nothing more. A kind of forest-born shopping – without money.

But of course, behind the threats of violence (they could and did kill) lay that same burning sense of injustice. The anger that drove them - and later the Socialists - to such extremes (like impromptu executions of nobility), was born of a psychological condition in which all hope of a decent future had been drained. And it could often be touched with an urge for revenge.

For instance the *pirali* Besarion Sikharulidze began his career as a peasant working for a village priest. But when the priest repeatedly failed to pay the eight roubles of wages he owed (quite a sum in those days), the desperate man eventually confronted the priest on the road with his demand. The priest flatly refused to pay, saying Besarion never worked hard enough to earn it, then threatened to call the police. At this point the peasant lost his temper and shot the priest dead. Thus Sikharulidze also became a forest *pirali*.

But the outlaw's day to day life is less romantic. Most had messy, violent and fairly short lives. Rarely did bandit careers last more than five years. Sometimes they'd be found and killed within months – either by the police or local vigilante groups out for the posted rewards.

But in Guria a good proportion of the peasantry supported these outlaws – not only for their wealth redistribution, but also for their ethics in the climate of endless cheating and stealing. This led to their assistance in the murder of many bounty-hunters – sent to eliminate the *pirali*, and a culture of silence developing among villagers. The kind that had caught up Gogia.

In many Gurian villages housewives regularly prepared extra food at supper-time: two portions set aside, in case a Sikharulidze or two dropped by. Often peasants were secretly grateful for the robberies, even assassinations, as the spoils were usually shared among them. This in spite of the fact some would later be forced to pay fines for covertly supporting outlaws. A fact that only hardened their commitment.

It was thanks mainly to this local encouragement that the Gurian Republic slowly developed - firstly through the creation of a tier system of elected local Committees (in which women had equal votes); then the setting up of 'People's Courts' and frequent 'People's Meetings.' Interestingly priests could often lead such gatherings, which sometimes carried a quasi-religious feel, with oaths sworn before crosses, or on the bible. Indeed the Social Democrats often accused the Gurian peasants and their Committees of being 'non-Marxist.' But they still couldn't help but admire the strong, collective spirit of these peasants, who the local Party then allowed to be re-categorised as 'workers' (rather than 'peasants' whom the Marxist Social Democrats considered incapable of political decision-making) and assisted in their organisation. By 1903 the Gurian Committees were functioning well and a kind of independent schooling system was developing, with Social Democrat-inclined teachers. This rapidly increased literacy in Guria and helped spread the revolutionary word. A culture of political debating was encouraged, where the writings of Marx, Lenin and Trotsky were earnestly discussed. This soon helped the peasants find the courage to start demanding land directly from the nobility - to the slogan 'land belongs to those who work it.' To this end they started to organise strikes or boycotts of some landowners' land. Arrests were made by the authorities, but due to Guria's remoteness in the Empire, not enough, and the peasants responded with strikes or terror tactics via their *pirali* - which proved quite effective.

It wasn't long before the peasants, backed by a communal sense of justice from their village meetings or 'circles,' started acting independently by confiscating the land; then farming the fields and orchards for themselves. Again these actions were organised and agreed by the village Committees, then enforced or appropriated with help from *pirali.* Some nobility even supported and partook in the Committees.

The whole organic structure of this extraordinary religio/Marxist Republic is described in more detail in Professor Stephen Jones's book *Socialism in Georgian Colours.*

Naturally some of the Georgian nobility and their Russian military friends, fought back. But not with sufficient vigour. Occasionally this would lead to village shoot-outs, sometimes in broad daylight, as in the American Wild West.

Take the time when Gogia Lomjaria and his friend Datulia were cornered by the notorious bounty-hunter, Captain Ivane Dumbadze and his troops. Apparently villagers crouched excitedly behind windows to watch the battle - that ended with Datulia riddled with bullets and dead, and a wounded Gogia escaping.

But like most things Gurian, the ambush contained more than met the eye. There is a saying in Guria - 'a second motive usually lies behind the first.' A state in which the highly complex, intertwining allegiances are almost impossible to unravel. Suffice to say, Captain Dumbadze had higher bosses to please – like the state's bounty-hunter-chief, Prince Gurieli, probably the wealthiest man in Guria.

A fact made all the more convoluted because Dumbadze had recently abducted the Prince's daughter and married her - a tradition then still tolerated in the Caucasus. While this naturally infuriated the Prince, it placed him in a difficult position. Without doubt the simplest solution would be - dispatch Dumbadze to join Datulia.

A Gurian Prince, taken by the Georgian photographer, Alex Roinishvili (1848-98)

Adding to the complexity yet again, were rumours that Gurieli had in fact struck a deal with Datulia and Gogia – to kill Dumbadze in the village battle, thus releasing his daughter from the bondage of marriage to a bounty-seeking thug. Which of course in the end failed.

This alliance may seem hard to believe - outlaws rarely cooperated with the authorities, especially those hunting them like Prince Gurieli. But in truth nobody knows the details of the deal, or even if there was one. And it has to be said *pirali* did sometimes visit, even stay in the homes of local nobility. It could have been because Social Democratic ideas were by now spreading in all directions – including upwards.

The degree of this is mostly speculation. But there can be no doubt, the extent of Guria's primary export - intrigue - could easily match any in Georgia. And it was from this ground of double-dealing, corruption, kidnapping and thievery, that the conspirators of the Gurian Republic found plenty of friends and sympathy in their desperate search for a way out. Tired of this merry-go-round of dishonesty, more and more people felt the urge to begin something completely new and more fair. Ironically, or perhaps not ironically, bandits would take a leading role in its creation.

By the early 20th century, this instinct had seeped deeply into the region's villages and towns. Because Guria was so poor and insignificant to the Empire, tucked away in its south western corner, it attracted less attention from the Cossacks and their beady-eyed administrators - so well described by the likes of Nikolai Gogol and Fyodor Dostoyevsky. The ideas of communal, rather than Russian justice were more able to infiltrate local structures.

As for the *pirali* themselves, by the beginning of the 20th century they'd become committed supporters of the incipient Socialist movement, prominent in policing and military operations in the evolving Republic. Gradually their tasks formalised into a kind of non-uniformed, paramilitary police force acting as official supporters of the poor. Soon local Social Democratic Councils, or Revolutionary Committees began to develop, to whom the *pirali* reported. Increasingly they found themselves fighting as much against robbery as carrying it out, confronting the other, more traditional bandits, face to face. Due to Guria's ongoing poverty there was still no shortage of thievery. But the *pirali* felt a corresponding sense of natural justice backing their actions - which could be very severe, even vicious. And it wouldn't be long before some of the more extreme among them started carrying out summary executions of the nobility.

Thus at the very beginnings of modern, applied Socialism, one can see the future divisions of character forming. Put simply, on one side the more easy-going, liberal in tone Mensheviks, and on the other, the harsher, more strident, militaristic Bolsheviks – who would finally devour the former in 1921 Georgia. Steadily some of the *pirali* groups of Guria would become ruthless or Bolshevik in enforcement of what would eventually be termed, 'the dictatorship of the proletariat.'

But such intellectual justifications of brutality would come later. Although it does show how personal psychology effects the broader spread of a national character, and can have strong bearing on the creation of political movements.

Gradually the Republic began to coalesce into a curious, slightly surreal partnership with the existing Russian administration. While the St Petersburg-loyal apparatchiks still sat behind their desks holding onto their positions and salaries, the town and village people's Committees steadily took away power – aided by their *pirali* police force. At first it became a parallel administration, then *the* administration, with the Russian appointed officers doing less and less in their offices. Some would say, continuing what they did anyway.

By 1902-03 Guria was turning more into a self-governing region, strongly guided by the increasingly fashionable Menshevik principles - expounded by those like Leon Trotsky (then a Menshevik, though he later switched to the Bolsheviks). Their leader, whom they called President, would become Benjamin (Benia) Chkhikvishvili. With a reputation for both bravery and thoughtful generosity, this dedicated Menshevik would later become mayor of Tbilisi, after the Social Democrats came to power in Georgia (1918). Later Benia returned from Paris to lead the failed 1924 rebellion against the Bolsheviks. He was captured, taken to Russia, shot, then they say, tossed from a moving train somewhere en route to Siberia.

As for the fates of our original *pirali,* - the trail-blazers - most also met sticky ends. After many fruitless attempts at capturing Gogia Lomjaria, Captain Dumbadze convinced the Kutaisi Gubernia authorities that this *pirali* was dangerous enough to justify a special punitive expedition to his home village.

Such techniques of punishing entire communities were then rare, due to their cruelty and blatant unfairness (though in 1923, after the Bolsheviks came to power, this became common practice). An armed Cossack brigade was moved into Gogia's neighbours' houses, where they ate and drank for free, extorting money, described as 'fines'. Although the villagers heroically complied and never sold Gogia out, the *pirali* began to feel ever more responsible. Finally he gave in, sent a letter to the Governor General in Kutaisi, offering to surrender if they recalled the Cossacks. When the Cossacks then left his village, Gogia turned himself in.

Possibly part of the deal was that he wasn't sent to Siberia. For after his trial he ended up in Kutaisi prison – then widely thought to be impregnable. But not for *pirali*. After two and a half years behind bars, Gogia Lomjaria decided time had come to officially end his *pirali* career, become a peasant again, and focus on providing for his family.

So he escaped - with a little inside help.

Captain Dumbadze - privately happy about another large bounty abruptly landing on Gogia's head, started to chase him again - from one end of Guria to the other. So Gogia moved to Adjara to join many other impoverished Gurian peasants working the land, sending money back to their families.

But it wasn't long before locals discovered Gogia Lomjaria's true identity, along with the reward. Wishing to claim some of it, the local Dadiani-Ogli family - local Muslim nobility - nabbed Gogia, arranged to hand him over to Captain Dumbadze in Kobuleti. But en-route to the rendez-vous Gogia struggled free, grabbed a guard's dagger, stabbed him and wounded two others. With their bounty now escaping his captors turned their guns on him and mistakenly killed him.

Thus the much-wanted outlaw arrived in Kobuleti as a corpse. The less-than-pleased Dumbadze – whose bounty had shrunk for delivering a dead rather than live outlaw - then tied Gogia's body to a tree trunk and fired several bullets from five steps away, to imitate a shoot-out. Turning to the captors, he abruptly accused them of sheltering a wanted criminal – hoping to claim their section of the reward.

Meanwhile news was sent to publications such as *Iveria,* declaring the notorious robber Gogia Lomjaria was dead; that peace would soon be returning to the troubled Gurian province.

CHAPTER 12

But unfortunately for Dumbadze, his dishonesty and fake bullets didn't work. The Dadiani-Ogli family protested loudly to the head of the Gubernia, explaining exactly what had happened. This ended Captain Dumbadze's career in Georgia. He was sent to Odessa along with his wife, Prince Gurieli's daughter, there to continue loyal service with the Empire.

But back in Guria, a kind of peace did finally arrive in the province. Or at least a form of more realistic justice - the kind depending on the removal from its soil of people like Captain Dumbadze. But in Guria they went one step better. And if one wanted to be hyperbolic, it could be added 'on behalf of International Socialism' - by organising the first practical application of Social Democracy's grand ideals into a living, functioning society.

And it lasted until 1906 - when after the failed, first Russian Revolution, the Tsar became extremely serious about wiping out every smallest sign of any potential Revolution.

It would take another twelve years to appear again. But when it did, it took over the entire country, turning it into the historic Georgian Democratic Republic, 1918-21.

Chapter 13

Pictures of a Revolution

After the First Russian Revolution of 1905-07 in St Petersburg, the unique Gurian Republic was stamped mercilessly out of existence. A Cossack army arrived under the leadership of General Alikhanov and wiped out the community courts, Committees, and as many *pirali* units as possible. For good measure they started a campaign of torching western Georgian villages, then roamed systematically around the Caucasus inflicting terrible vengeance on all Revolutionaries. As a result Georgia would never be what Alexandre Jambakur-Orbeliani had hoped. Neither what Ilia Chavchavadze had dreamed – though by then Ilia was dead - killed by guerrillas in 1907 on the directives of a People's Committee. An organisation he himself indirectly midwifed into existence.

Guerrillas. Directives. People's Committee - hitherto unknown words in Georgia.

They belonged to the new Revolutionary country now emerging, piggybacking on political events in its giant neighbour to the north - for the moment driven back underground by General Alikhanov. But the fire of Revolutionary thought hadn't gone away - having already swept down through Russia, crossing the Caucasus mountains and changing Georgian politics forever. While the First Russian Revolution had failed physically, it hadn't mentally – at all. The Georgia of old, where one's word carried more weight than one's signature, was fully gone - consigned to the summary executions of history.

Up north, Georgia's contribution to the Russian Revolution was surprisingly large – aided of course, by figures like Stalin. With the experience of the Gurian Republic fresh in their minds, Georgia moved instinctively toward the Menshevik end of the Revolutionary spectrum - led by prominent Gurian Social Democrats like Noe Ramishvili (1881-1930), later the Chairman of the Independent Georgian Government, and

Noe Jordania, who took over until its eradication by the Bolsheviks in 1921.

But the new Tsarist repressions couldn't wipe out the Committees. They simply became more secretive - participants remaining resolutely faithful to the communal purpose. Pseudonyms became de-rigueur. Symbols, codes, information gleaning/stealing, assassination, arrest, escape - daily life for both sides. It created an accompanying fear of infiltration, spies, fifth columnists - a kind of heroic paranoia establishing itself in the growing ranks of Social Democrat activists. Mentally looking over one's shoulder became a standard reflex – which after the Bolshevik/Soviet take-over in 1917 could determine one's life or death. But always still tinged with that redoubtable Georgian optimism.

As for that centuries-old refuge for Georgian identity and character, the church - the former nationalist Revolutionaries were changing their opinion. Since Russia's official colonisation of Georgia in 1801, the icons and even some liturgy had become Russianised. The church structures were officially absorbed, then subordinated into those of the Russian Orthodox Patriarchy. The church became increasingly an imperial instrument. Independence seekers like Ilia Chavchavadze, distrusted its priests. Gradually the local religion was turning not only into 'the opium of the people,' but a Tsarist thought-prison out of which any true Georgian Social Democrat had to escape.

Now was the time of the new Socialist materialists like Datiko Shevardnadze: originally a young *pirali* of the Gurian forests, then one of the original 'Red Guerrillas,' (or 'Red Detachments' - their more polite Revolutionary term). These evolved from the *pirali*, and protected, as Datiko saw it, the dignity of his native Ploughmen and Sowers, soldiering gallantly against the Empire.

There were many others like him across Georgia. Ironically Ilia Chavchavadze's killers were almost certainly also Red Guerrillas, but it is said from Kartli. Not professional Revolutionaries, just eager supporters of their noble Social Democratic cause. These soon would become its foot-soldiers, more on Lenin's Bolshevik side of the Russian Social Democratic Labour Party, after it split with the Mensheviks.

To them Ilia Chavchavadze increasingly became a kind of bank-owning, bourgeois and nationalist romantic – an 'enemy' to their Revolution. And the Bolsheviks loved creating enemies. Ilia's disapproval of the Red Guerrillas and his strong influence on the general public was seen as a barrier to be eliminated on their road to power.

But of course, the Red Guerrillas themselves came in many shades of commitment. From the bright crimson of dedicated political terrorists, to the rusty red of modified robbers discovering a cause. Later on came the pinkishness of a good many fairly ordinary young people, swept up in the gathering nationalist zeal, borne on the ideals of independence. It should also be mentioned that other factions in Georgian politics - the Anarchists, Social Federalists, right-wing patriots, also operated guerrillas, sometimes even shared them (like the Mensheviks and Bolsheviks until mid 1907).

Stepping back, the national character seemed to be entering a period of change - again. Society was polarising, and the opposing sides hardening in their attitudes. To examine this more closely, it's worth considering Datiko Shevardnadze's evolving career.

Born in 1875 to a peasant family, he stood out from other fighters as one of the better educated and travelled. He even made it as far as Novorossiysk in southern Russia, where he worked as a foreman on the docks. On his return he became a village scribe, office-bound, transcribing documents. Not a demanding position, nor giving much back in salary. Like many others in his profession he supported the Social Democrats. And egged-on by their idealism, the job soon began to feel way too status-quo. Just sitting in his office, writing and re-writing useless circulars with neat handwriting. No wonder he began breaking the rules, assisting village peasants, even creating false documents.

In evenings and weekends, once free from the office, he continued to work on his favourite pastime – perfecting the art of over-the-shoulder shooting on horseback. He would soon become one of Guria's best. A kind of early 20th century Clark Kent (of *Superman* fame), spending his daytimes shuffling administrative papers, then at night pulling open his shirt and developing his get-away marksmanship.

By and by he began to cooperate more and more with the Social Democrats, who spotting his *pirali*-style talents, soon called on him to carry out actions that today would be termed terrorism. Even without the Revolution, many Gurian outlaws ruthlessly persecuted those working for the authorities, spies in particular. And their methods included murder, or as they saw it justified execution - which would soon become almost industrial across the Empire. Bomb factories were already springing up in Tbilisi, (or Tiflis as it was then called), and in the year leading to mid 1906, Georgian police estimated about one political assassination every three days. This growing violence left Datiko's standing with the Party slightly awkward. A bit too blood-thirsty to be openly praised... but still useful, and in many ways.

One of these uses was for the clandestine transportation of key Party officials and propagandists, as the Revolutionaries set out, ever more successfully, to spread their word. The favourite Social Democratic vehicle for this was the hay cart. Which is how Datiko became friends with one Joseph Jugashvili (1878-1953), then known as Koba, (subsequently adopting the surname, Stalin). Datiko's association with the future Soviet leader began as conversations while they banged along the road, Stalin peering out from under Datiko's mountain of hay. Later Stalin would praise this Gurian Red Guerrilla, citing not only his bravery and tactics, but lawless, over-the-shoulder sense of humour – as a key Revolutionary ingredient.

As the *pirali* militias grew in size and prominence, their roles edged toward what might be labelled small-scale death squads – Socialist variety, acting on the directives of village Committees. As the calls for revolution grew louder, so the Russian Empire's borderlands in Georgia, became even more like the American Wild-West – but with an important difference. Instead of an atmosphere of lone and fierce individualism where the law faced the easier task of dealing with self-serving outlaws and thieves – here it faced a gathering, organised force of idealistic law-breakers hell-bent on taking over the government itself.

On one occasion Datiko and fellow bandit, Gogitidze (Christian names were often not recorded in Georgian historical documents), were sent to assassinate a suspected spy for the Empire. Failing to track him down, they adjourned their mission at a roadside tavern. After a good many drinks, they rode off singing loudly and, so the story goes, horribly out of tune. Along the way they encountered another Gurian Red Guerrilla called Makharadze, who it turned out, had formerly 'justifiably executed' Datiko's godfather.

Consequently the three activists, who already knew each other, faced-off on a deserted road. Makharadze was soon mocking their awful singing and a heated argument quickly developed. With all the participants habitual killers, soon only one resolution remained - the death of one. Which, as it happened, would be Makharadze - shot dead by Gogitidze.

This prompted an investigation by the Party itself. But due to its haphazard and arbitrary methodology, Datiko suddenly found himself being accused of avenging his godfather's death. In spite of his protests, he found himself facing the very assassination sentence he'd usually be charged to carry out. Thus he became a wanted man by his own comrades. But by now any form of reliable justice was becoming a thing of the past. An increasingly chaotic and bloody atmosphere was starting to infect Georgia in the decade leading up to the 1917 Revolution in St Petersburg, when the Tsar himself ended-up among the executed.

With his name openly declared public enemy number one in Guria, Datiko Shevardnadze found even the Socialist-leaning newspapers reporting on every attempt to eliminate him. Because the Red Guerrilla identities were carefully guarded, the editors remained fully unaware of his Socialist commitment.

But spies were everywhere in Guria, and on every side. Soon word reached the Governor-General of the Socialist's intention to eliminate their former activist. So he arranged a secret meeting with Datiko in Ozurgeti, the region's capital, believing he'd be happy to divulge a few names of those hunting him. But the former village scribe, true to his hidden Socialist colours, never grassed on anyone.

Around this time the Social Democrats hired an assassin, known as Basilia, to take Datiko out. After some hunting, Basilia finally tracked him down in a village centre. Choosing his moment, he stepped forward and raised his pistol, as watching villagers ducked behind window-frames. But instead of confronting his attacker with his own pistol, the wanted superhero turned and ran, simultaneously aiming a single shot back over his shoulder. Due to his years of practice, it hit and wounded Basilia. The village constable arrived shortly, but to everyone's surprise Datiko re-appeared, explaining they'd both been attacked by bandits and Basilia had unfortunately caught a bullet. A clear demonstration of Datiko's ongoing loyalty to the Party - surprisingly common among Revolutionaries.

Not so long after these two demonstrations of Socialist commitment, the Party exonerated him within their own structures, re-admitted him back to the cause – not only as a highly effective and ruthless fighter, but one of the Red Guerrilla commanders.

And he proved himself well. So much so that when the Cossacks were sent into Guria to deal with the Social Democrat rebels at a show-down in Nasakirali village (2nd November, 1905), Datiko organised the Red Guerrillas so effectively the Cossacks were sent scampering for their lives.

Datiko's reputation continued to grow, to the degree he carried sufficient authority to force local constables, or officers of the Empire, to change tactics – several times making them abandon punitive village assaults, on pain of his personal retribution. His voice, everyone said, was becoming louder than his gun. Meanwhile Socialist numbers grew steadily across the Caucasus.

As for the new generation of young men in Guria, the region still offered very few serious career opportunities. The ambitious either joined the Imperial gendarmerie or became Revolutionaries. The former ensured a police or military career, a medal or two and regular salary, the latter, heroic life as an outlaw. Conformity, predictable police work and income - versus nothing predictable, mostly poverty (though not always), but a noble cause.

No surprise then that Red Guerrilla also numbers swelled in the years leading up to Europe's WWI.

Meanwhile the Russian army repressions served only to motivate locals even more toward the Social Democrats, who were by now organising new trade unions, people's universities, newspapers and strikes. A soft civil war that after the Bolshevik take-over in 1921 and the Russian Civil War, would turn very hard.

As one of their poster-boys, Datiko's reputation soon grew into that of bullet-proof superhero and serious thorn in the side of the authorities. Furthermore he never missed an opportunity to prove it – especially when any young-blood gendarme announced intentions to deliver Datiko in a box.

Like one Platon Kalandadze, the eldest of three Gurian police brothers. On hearing this Datiko hurried straight over to the Kalandadze house to ask Platon face to face, if he still really meant it. But the house was empty save for the brothers' elderly mother. So the Red Guerrilla delivered Platon a message - in the form of twenty bullets fired straight into his empty bed. The kind of technique his friend Stalin would no doubt have approved – though with occupied beds.

CHARACTER in Georgia

Stalin with his daughter Svetlana. This image of the man of steel wasn't released until long after his death, in Perestroika time.

But still, if the determination was strong enough in the authorities, even bullet-proof superheroes couldn't last in the Gurian Wild West. 'The law' had other ways of dealing with criminals and terrorists – beyond their own rules.

The growing network of Red Guerrillas like Datiko, depended for their survival and sustenance on locals. If the authorities dug deep and paid well enough, they could usually find someone willing to betray a bandit in a discreet, less-identifiable way - like poisoning. A fact made all the easier by this Red Guerrilla's habit of changing locations up to five times a night – thereby providing numerous possible betrayers.

As the story goes, Datiko Shevardnadze's life was ended by police poison, supplied to a potential host in advance. Apparently after eating the spiked meal, he stumbled around for a few days, then just to end the pain, identified himself to soldiers or *chapari*, who promptly shot him dead.

But his death didn't stop the wave of revolutionary attacks or terror. Indeed shortly afterwards his friend Kikia Mamulaishvili made a point of avenging his death by organising a Red Guerrilla

CHAPTER 13

attack on Datiko's local police station. They killed two officers, including Platon Kalandadze. Apparently they then rode over to Datiko's grave, fired a military salute into the air and loudly sang the *Marseillaise* – in tune.

The Revolution of course, was a far bigger process than mere guerrilla attacks in Guria. For a grander picture we might turn our eyes towards Georgia's second city, Kutaisi; sniff the thickening Socialist air. After all, according to Marxist theory, it would be the urban revolutionaries that would ultimately lead the peasants to the victory of the proletariat.

Certainly when any young man felt the revolutionary urge in a city environment, it was pretty obvious that fighting alone, bandit-style, would achieve little. Nor was it enough just to become a Party member. Without help and support from the local community, any revolutionary acts could fizzle. People at all levels had to be cultivated. The Party could help provide a structure and some general organisation - as in the Gurian Republic Committees. But in the new, heavily policed atmosphere of post 1907 Georgia, the Social Democrats were still in the stage of re-grouping and capable of only small local coups.

Clandestine presses and newspapers began to appear – and disappear. Some like *The Social Democrat*, published articles by dedicated scholars/Revolutionaries such as Noe Ramishvili – often from out of the country. Pen-names could be life-savers. Having been banned from Georgia and forced into exile - Ramishvili spent time in London and Germany – the Tsarist police at home describing him as 'the father of terror.' But exiled Revolutionaries often crept back in under false names and passports – until captured again. Noe Jordania was stuck in Italy when Ilia Chavchavadze was murdered. But as for his opinion on the event? He would famously quote the phrase used when the French Revolutionaries beheaded the esteemed chemist and nobleman Antoine Lavoisier;

'Splinters will fly when wood has to be chopped.'

The propaganda operation was in full flow – right across Europe. Activists were busily stitching together well-linked networks, infiltrating ever deeper into town and city structures, at every level. Hands-on operatives, like Stalin and his many cart-trips, were having influence, not only across the Caucasus, but Russia as well.

Noe Jordania

With the repressions following the failed 1905 Russian Revolution in full swing across Georgia, Social Democrats were systematically sought out and arrested. Some were just shot, but a good many sentenced to long periods out of harm's way in Siberia. Due to the growing number of grass-roots supporters, many Mensheviks managed to escape en route. Some from their mustering point - Kutaisi prison – mostly by bribing guards. Others devised ways of curtailing long sentences – by switching places with lesser criminals or making a dash for it during transportation across the Russian steppe.

CHAPTER 13

All this required good inside help and information. Baron Bibineishvili, who later became a Bolshevik, remembered receiving instructions from Party superiors on how to observe and cultivate new recruits;

1) Identify the potential comrade.
2) Learn their habits.
3) Befriend them systematically.
4) Gently glean information.
5) Wean them over to the Party.

The most common targets were clerks and low-ranking officials in government offices. Very handy when Revolutionaries needed passports, clean ones for travel across the Empire or abroad. This would ideally require a genuine, blank document which could then be filled in with a new, substituted name. Revolutionaries needed many aliases and the poorly made fake passports with substituted photos were all too easy to spot at Georgia's many military checkpoints on its road network.

A good example of the process is with the new recruit Alpez Museridze, a young clerk in the Kutaisi Gubernia Secretariat. Identified as a possible sympathiser with an ability to supply documents, he was first invited to a restaurant. If that went well - it did - he received a second invitation. With his allegiance confirmed, financial incentives would normally be offered – money supplied by the many *pirali*, or Red Guerrilla robberies. But Museridze is said to have cooperated without payment. The next important step came in convincing the young clerk to provide a list of those waiting for new passports. Names of real people were essential, because the authorities sometimes checked if the name on the arrested person's passport, actually existed. If it didn't, troubles promptly doubled.

But even with the list, success wasn't always guaranteed - as in the case of a young Revolutionary detained in Baku. His identity document claimed he lived in Kutaisi. But when his name was checked with Kutaisi police, the young activist turned out to be an elderly priest.

Or the successes - as when a key Georgian Revolutionary was arrested in St Petersburg. The Russian police believed him a very different person to one named in his passport – which he definitely was. So they contacted Kutaisi police for verification. But the Kutaisi Social Democratic Committee, through their elaborate network of informers, also heard about the check and managed to locate the family of the person used on the fake passport. To their horror they discovered the man on the fake passport was already under arrest and exiled in Siberia.

After some quick thinking, members of the Committee approached the prisoner's elderly father with an idea. When the arrested Revolutionary was returned to Kutaisi for trial - for escaping from Siberia – the Committee staged an elaborate piece of theatre for the still suspicious authorities. As soon as the mock father and son saw each other, the old man ran up and hugged the young man - whom he'd never seen before – thus confirming his identity to the authorities. The trial was then held, the fake Siberian escapee reconvicted and transferred to Kutaisi prison – from where he of course, escaped. Thus the Revolution continued - with such escape cases multiplied by the thousands. Stalin was a great master of the art – escaping they say, at least seven times.

It might be noted that during the First Russian Revolution (1905-07), the majority of Committee members in Tbilisi and Batumi were Mensheviks. But in Kutaisi Bolsheviks dominated – setting a more violent tone to operations. Indeed Stalin would soon operate several Red Guerrilla units out of the city. Revolutionaries even managed to enlist the assistance of the Head of the District's wife (Head of District is akin to Head of Town or Parish Council, with strong military connections, especially in Kutaisi).

This pointed to another fact helping the Revolutionary cause. Some of the more discerning nobility, sniffing a major social change, made discreet overtures towards the Social Democrats. Initially many were just out to protect their assets, but in so doing initiated a similar kind of infiltration of the Revolutionaries. First there'd be invitations - perhaps even a restaurant. Then they'd see if their chosen rebels might be bribable. If not they'd begin a sly cosying-up and befriending of the enemy. But in so doing they inadvertently absorbed some of the Social Democratic ideas. And some stuck. For as we shall see later, some nobility in Georgia happily gave up most of their estates for redistribution to the peasants, after 1918.

Set between these political extremes lay another large and significant part of the population - whose voices are usually missed by history. The nice, law-abiding mass of ordinary people and middle classes.

CHAPTER 13

In Kutaisi they might be personified by the mild-mannered Varlam Pantskhava – a liberal educationalist. He came to notice only because he lived in a largish house with a walled garden directly across from Kutaisi prison (no longer existing today). Soon he found himself being harassed by Revolutionary's families asking if they might climb to his second-story, then shout over to their loved ones, stuck behind bars in the adjacent prison. Being an obliging man, he agreed. But when the authorities noticed, they demanded that Pantskhava cover his windows and not allow anyone onto his balcony.

This he was naturally reluctant to do. For if he complied, the poor man faced worse reprisals from the Revolutionaries. This left the authorities facing a problem, for they'd no law to compel him to obey. So the prison administration finally resorted to covering their own second story windows with metal sheets.

It wasn't long afterwards that a well-dressed man arrived at Varlam's door with a generous business proposal. Could he rent Varlam's house to allow his wife and his sister-in-law to set up their weaving workshop? Pantskhava's house apparently possessed all the right rooms and facilities for a successful business.

Happy for the chance to move away from the harassment of prisoner's families, he agreed. Soon the new tenants were hanging colourful carpets, cardigans and socks out in the garden. Splashes of colour that pleased everyone, even the prison administration. Customers came and went, a good many, buying the fabrics. All seemed to be going well.

Except they were also digging a tunnel into the prison. The respectable, well-dressed man had been a member of the Kutaisi Bolshevik committee; his 'wife,' Eremia Lomtatidze, a dedicated Revolutionary. The tunnel was started in Varlam's basement and was to emerge in a carefully chosen ground floor 'Recreational Room' in the prison, close to where inmates exercised during the prison regime. Incidentally a regime much milder than the one later imposed by the same Bolsheviks, after they took over Kutaisi jail in 1921.

But the tunnel was long and complicated, so two miners had to be brought in from the Chiatura manganese mine, via the local Party. They redesigned it, then set up a rota of ten people working in shifts.

Soon 37 inmates, mainly Bolsheviks, were selected for the grand escape. The plan was to use a complex signalling system, leading them into the Recreational Room one by one. Then they'd quickly jump into the tunnel and crawl away to freedom in a series of pre-arranged safe-houses – located by Baron Bibineishvili.

Of course, with so many links in this complicated chain, any one failure would collapse the whole process - with disastrous consequences all round. But the Committee members were good organisers. For instance, when Pantskhava made an unannounced visit to his rental property and discovered a crowd of miners digging a hole in his basement, he was given a sizeable sum to keep quiet. Which he did.

And so on the 25th of September 1907, 37 inmates trooped one by one from the exercise yard into the Recreational Room – and never re-emerged. Every one made their way through the tunnel to Pantskhava's basement. After a rapid change of clothes, they were taken to the safe houses to lie low for a couple of days, before any attempts were made to leave Kutaisi. All exit points were being rigorously checked by the infuriated police. The selected homes belonged to a wide variety of people. One deacon by the name of Kandelaki, hid Lenin's friend Davit Suliashvili (who'd met the Soviet leader in exile abroad). Badua Chikovani, the secretary of the Governor-General concealed Moses Beitler, a Jewish supporter of the revolution then on death-row, actually in the attic of the Governor General's house.

The whole city seemed to be involved in the conspiracy to hide the escapees. About ten of them were cared for by 'ladies,' including the wife of the Head of District. A barber and hairdresser were employed to provided wigs and radical new haircuts (Stalin once successfully disguised himself as a woman in one of his escapes,). Fake passports were quickly prepared and slowly the escapees ventured out of Kutaisi, via different routes. But strangely, the majority were then re-captured – mostly at the railway station.

There was a reason for this - discovered when Moses Beitler immediately found himself recaptured in his railway carriage - in a way suggesting the police knew in advance. Suddenly the escape-master, Alpez Museridze came under suspicion. His charges were too frequently being arrested, but never himself. The Committee members began to wonder if his dapper 'cover' appearance, was in fact the sign of his true loyalty – to the authorities.

CHAPTER 13

To test his loyalty Bibineishvili then set a trap for Museridze, by sharing some fake 'secret' information about moving escapees to a new safe-house.

The house was promptly raided - to find no prisoners. Since it could have been a coincidence – houses were raided constantly - they told Museridze of another new, fake safe-house. Another raid promptly happened and the Revolutionaries reluctantly concluded Museridze had turned. Switching allegiances did happen - and both ways. In fact Museridze had been offered a major promotion – as Chief Constable of Tkibuli.

Meanwhile Bibineishvili noticed another strange fact about Museridze. Any Revolutionary shaking his hand during walks around Kutaisi's streets, was too often arrested shortly afterwards. A hidden signal perhaps to some following secret police?

So spotting Museridze on the Boulevard, Bibineishvili walked straight up and boldly stretched out a hand. Museridze at first just stared at his fellow conspirator sensing something was up, but had no option than to shake his hand. Once Museridze was out of sight, Bibineishvili was promptly arrested by the over-eager following police – who were indeed watching. But this time, Museridze mysteriously re-appeared and convinced the soldiers to release his friend - no doubt intending to restore his cover.

But now the cat was fully out the bag. Bibineishvili's revolutionary colleagues quickly hired an assassin. Museridze must have sensed it, for he started walking around town with a six-soldier escort. But one day, when making a quick, solo visit to a bookshop, the assassin stepped forward and shot the future Police Chief dead.

And so the assassinations increased. Even Baron Bibineishvili became a murderer – perhaps taking his lead from the Museridze betrayal, and shortly afterwards gunned down the Secret Police Chief right there on the Boulevard.

As mentioned, like elsewhere in the Russian Empire, Georgia teemed with many versions of the Revolutionary, or those seeking radical political change. By the time of the First World War they had divided into many camps. Apart from the original Social Democrats, who split into the Mensheviks and Bolsheviks in 1903, there were also the Socialist Revolutionaries, Left Socialist Revolutionary Party, Social Federalists,

Menshevik Internationalists, Constitutional Monarchists, Anarchists, to name a few. Baron Bibineishvili ended up as a hard-core Bolshevik following Lenin – who's policies in the chaos of Russia's Revolutionary politics, ultimately prevailed. But other character-types also dreamed of independence from Russia in Georgia. This meant other methods of achieving the same goal - particularly when it came to financing the Revolution.

A number of mafia-esque figures and white-collar criminals would discover new energy for their activities under the Socialist Revolutionary or Social Federalist flags.

One such was Paliko Kipiani, who emerged out of the Caucasian underworld and ran off to Europe with 26,000 roubles from the Baku branch of Georgia's Nobility Bank. Never that active in the Georgian Revolutionary movement, he did still help finance the publication of a Georgian-language newspaper in France, but only while developing a handy side-line as arms dealer.

Once in Paris he tracked down some of the Revolutionaries, including the Social Federalist, Giorgi Dekanozishvili, who wanted to organise an arms shipment to his motherland. He put Kipiani in touch with the well-known Georgian millionaire and philanthropist Iakob Zubalashvili, then living in one of the city's more expensive hotels.

'Our comrades require 25,000 roubles in gold,' Kipiani then demanded from Zubalishvili. For some reason the millionaire agreed.

It's not known exactly why. Possibly Kipiani discovered some of the philanthropist's underhand dealings and blackmailed him with disclosure. Perhaps the financier also wanted Georgian independence. The Zubalashvili brothers were much respected philanthropists and not all revolutionaries approved of Kipiani's methods. Either way most of the money went on a reported 7,000 Swiss rifles and a million bullets, to be shipped to Georgia in the autumn of 1905. This ended up as a story in itself.

Once the weapons were purchased a ship had to be found. Eventually, with the help of a Dutch anarchist, the Sirius, a Swedish built freighter, was hired from the Japanese (then at war with Russia), and loaded under the disapproving eyes of the French port authorities.

But who would sail it? Working as a gun-runner to a potentially Revolutionary country, wasn't choice employment. Fortunately for them, more Anarchists came to the rescue again. Twenty, mostly French and Dutch, were hired and the boat finally set sail for Poti.

But with Poti being in Georgia, gossip arrived in advance of the ship. Once spotted on the horizon, a crowd of Revolutionaries assembled in the harbour to welcome the rifles into the homeland. As the first batch landed on-shore, the local Social Federalists inspected them eagerly - finding the guns different and better than those of the Russians. But too eagerly it turned out, as one was accidentally fired. Next thing the dock was swarming with police and port authorities, who were soon rowing out to the foreign ship. Seeing their approach, the crew rapidly tossed the remaining rifles into the sea.

Apparently 3,000 still made it to Georgia - out of which the Social-Democrat revolutionaries received a few and the police, the rest. But even so, the shipment was hailed as a success - especially when compared to other attempts - as from countries like Finland and Poland.

As for how much those weapons helped Georgia free itself from the Russian Empire – no one will ever know.

As for their users; during the pre-Revolution, the Bolsheviks believed the natural rebellion of workers against their bosses would see them take up weapons and win the fight for Socialism. But the slightly less militaristic Menshevik Socialists - still the majority in Georgia, particularly Tbilisi - were happy enough to use them, just more nicely. Then there were the Revolutionaries not belonging to any party; but driven by romantic ideas of independence. Most too were prepared to bear arms - by then Stalin was permanently carrying a pistol. By the autumn of 1905, the many factions of revolutionary thought were mixing freely together across Georgia, living, working, striking, arguing endlessly amongst themselves. City streets became a blend of peasants, workers, middle-classes, theoreticians, terrorists, bandits, Red Guerrillas. Their activities included holding rallies, waving flags and banners, delivering passionate speeches, and sometimes simply going to work - all guided by a handful of charismatic leaders.

Out of them all, the Anarchists were perhaps most easily spotted, for their long hair and beards – following the creeds (and hairstyles) of Peter Kropotkin and Leo Tolstoy. In 1921 there was even a large Anarchist army controlling a significant part of Ukraine, referred to as the 'Blacks.' In Georgia they tended to act individually or in small groups, generally avoiding the common population - who they regarded as sadly misguided. But their utilitarian philosophy also allowed them to suddenly side with this or that party, as was expedient.

A good example of a Georgian Anarchist was Alexandre Gabunia; a short, agile man who found particular favour among the Revolutionaries – due to his skills as a chemist, thus bomb-maker. Then there was Davit Rostomashvili, an Anarchist-terrorist who felt no compunction at throwing them. Or Mikheil Kancheli who, although not a bomb-thrower, once hurled a beer keg at Leon Trotsky in Switzerland during a heated debate, declaring that since he wasn't any good at arguing, this was his answer. All these characters played decisive roles in the class-struggle/mini-civil war that was steadily consuming Georgia and the Russian Empire.

Bomb-throwing, robbery and assassination became a kind of routine across the Caucasus, where the terrorists employed increasingly complex techniques. For instance Valodia Goguadze, a decorated ex-soldier, would throw his bombs - initially in Baku - then quickly slap on his row of medals (all genuine), which included the St George Cross, and stride away proudly down the street. The police never suspected such a revered patriot.

Or the time when a police station received an anonymous letter identifying the hideout of the notorious bomb-thrower Rostomashvili. The police promptly raided the house, found no one, so initiated a deeper search. When the Chief Officer opened a cupboard in the bedroom, it exploded and killed him. Later it transpired that Rostomashvili had sent the letter himself.

As for the terrorists themselves, life became one dramatically gory event after another – revealed in their diaries and memoirs. As the bombs and hand-grenades began to run out, local 'factories' were needed. This is where the dense Gurian forest came into its own. The first bomb factory was well concealed deep inside, initially as just a hut, housing a small group of operatives - Alexandre Gabunia, Rezo Gabashvili, a blacksmith and some guards. But it marked the beginnings of a new industry for impoverished Guria - grenades.

Having previously taken control of Guria, the Social-Democrats were still influential. Locals already knew what it was like to slowly strip the power away from the priests, police and nobility, place it in the hands

CHAPTER 13

of their own Party committees and village 'circles.' The *pirali* remained active, endlessly forming new mini-militias to fight bogus Revolutionaries who used Socialism as an excuse to steal for themselves. This battle soon became almost as vicious as the one against the Cossacks.

On one occasion the *pirali* and former soldier Valodia Goguadze nearly lost his life while protecting a peasant's single cow from such thieves. Wounded in the knee, he spent eighteen months moving house to house across Guria, unable to find a surgeon. Eventually the peasant's traditional methods and herbal medicine saved his leg and life.

By now the world outside Georgia was undergoing its own upheaval. The First World War had started, the Germans were soon battling Britain. The Revolutionaries in Georgia watched the events anxiously, trying to figure out which side to support. Around 1915 some Revolutionaries met in Samtredia to discuss their options. One group decided to support Germany partly due to secret negotiations with German leaders, who offered independence to Georgia. However the Social Democrats didn't fully trust this option and sided with England. In this way Georgia created a perfect solution – if either side won, there would be local options to support both winners.

Meanwhile back on the ground, the Socialist Revolutionaries, Bolsheviks and Mensheviks needed ever more grenades. To stay one step ahead of the police, workshop locations were constantly changed. But concealment wasn't required only for bomb-factories. Gabunia and Gabashvili's hut was soon visited by two cash-bearing Party members, with a fresh order. This took place at night - deliberately - so nobody could see their faces. They were in fact Noe Ramishvili and a key activist code-named Itria.

As in many such cases the secrecy held – perhaps one reason why the Revolution ultimately succeeded. It was only in 1921 that Gabashvili finally rumbled Itria in Paris, recognising him solely from his handshake, due to Itria's unusually dry skin and missing finger (a common trope of bomb-handlers). In fact, Itria was the Party name for Vlasa Mgeladze – a much revered Revolutionary, who on Georgia's Independence Day, May 26th, 1918, rode up to St David's Church in Tbilisi, rang its bell, shouting down at the graves of Ilia Chavchavadze, Akaki Tseretali and Vazha Pshavela,

'Georgia's free, we did it!'

Early 20th century postcard showing St David's Church and Tbilisi's then new funicular

Certainly the romance and drama of revolution drew many into its fold. This applied as much to women as men. Nino Kipiani (1877-1920), the Russian Empire's first female lawyer and later a very talented writer in her own right, was arrested several times, then released. Once when her home was searched, the *Okhrana* (the Tsar's secret police) walked right past a handwritten note pinned to her wall: a childishly encrypted message from Giorgi Dekanozishvili in Europe, saying he'd sent over 'the apples and sticks' – apples being code for bombs and sticks, rifles. But after the raid Nino still didn't destroy the note – making it into a kind of talisman. Maybe it worked, for not long afterwards when walking with Rezo Gabashvili round Tbilisi's Metekhi prison (since removed), looking for suitable tunnel-exits near the church, the police decided they were acting suspiciously - which they were. Both were stopped and searched, but again the police failed to find the incriminating note, this time in Gabashvili's pocket. The couple simply walked on, part-confirming that eternal suspicion that successful revolutions are won (or lost) as much through blunders as clever tactics.

Then there is that even more devious technique - of pretending to make blunders. For this we might look at the case of one frequently arrested Georgian/Armenian revolutionary called Simon Ter-Petrosyan (1882-1922). Having fled the Empire after numerous imprisonments, arrests and escapes, he was finally picked up by German police in Berlin as a dangerous terrorist, on information from the Tsar's *Okhrana*. Once in the cell he started acting strangely. Fearing he might be on the edge of madness the authorities transferred him to the mental hospital. His medical records report him showing profound depression one day, elation the next. That he stripped himself naked, stopped talking, refused to eat, then for two months paced earnestly around his room, singing loudly, pulling out his hair. When asked if he was religious or having mystical experiences, he replied the world had only two Gods left - Marx and Engels; that he was in active debate with both. Finally a German psychiatrist concluded he was a hysteric of low intelligence and incapable of standing trial. The best solution would be, simply deport him back to his country of origin – Armenia.

The technique worked. Simon Ter-Petrosyan's country of origin was in fact Georgia. He spoke only a few Armenian words learned from his parents during his Gori childhood, after which he adopted his Party name of Kamo. He would go on to fool the authorities again with his madness technique – once even declaring it so successful he wondered if he might actually be mad.

Kamo - Bolshevik master of disguises, that included madness

CHARACTER in Georgia

Photo of Tbilisi's Metekhi church and prison, taken in the late 19th century. The prison was built by the Russian authorities mid 19th century to house the many rebels, nationalists then Social Democratic revolutionaries, fighting against the Empire. Stalin was one and is said to have received a good socialist education from his fellow inmates. Lavrenti Beria wanted the church pulled down in the 1930s, but it escaped by being repurposed as a theatre. The prison, possibly due to the number of escapes, was removed instead.

CHARACTER in Georgia

Kamo was only three years younger than Stalin, and they knew each other from Gori, where Stalin was also schooled. Indeed Stalin claimed that a blending of national-identities like Kamo's, proved that true Bolsheviks had no ethnicity. The Revolution belonged to a pan-cultural personality identifying solely with the 'collective will of the people.' A belief the Communists tried to impose by dissolving all the Soviet Union's internal ethnic borders. Ultimately this proved unsuccessful, as seen after its collapse in 1991, when the nationalities re-established themselves with terrible ferocity. Some say this illustrated Bolshevism's psychological immaturity - that doomed it to failure. Comparable perhaps to Marx's blunted claim that capitalism would eat itself via rampant competition and alienation.

Kamo became one of the Revolution's most prominent activists and soon a friend of Lenin. Initially he dreamed of a military career, but failing army admission, he, along with Baron Bibineishvili opted for accountancy.

Lenin, who liked Kamo, even offered him a private tutor. But academia wasn't his, nor Bibineishvili's forte – as the Revolution proved. Records show he travelled to 19 countries, much of the time incognito, mostly operating as a highly successful hands-on weapons and money mule.

Partly due to his ongoing acting talents, Kamo maintained a personal prop-wardrobe of favourite disguises. One was a low-ranking Russian military officer (possibly the one he never became) – though less convincing due to his small, non-athletic stature. Another was a Georgian noble. But closest to his heart was the character of a Tbilisi *kinto* – a street salesman, often in Armenian dress, recognisable by large trays or baskets carried on their heads. In normal circumstance they'd be laden with fruit, but Kamo's tray invariably concealed a layer of hand-grenades under the pomegranates.

When arrested in Germany, his suitcase was discovered crammed with hand-grenade-making materials. This makes his asylum performance all the more remarkable. Revolutionaries were hated across Europe. After his repatriation he was eventually transferred to Mikheil's Hospital in Tbilisi. Exactly the destination he wanted - a far easier escape-venue than prison. One of his two sisters – both Revolutionaries - bribed an orderly to deliver a metal-file to Kamo. Just as in the Chaplin films, he achieved freedom by sawing through the window-bars.

A kinto tradesman - one of Kamo's many disguises, often employed during hand-grenade distribution

In Soviet mythology Kamo was presented as a true Revolutionary 'hero' – though in reality he might be described as a typically blood-thirsty Bolshevik. Certainly his number of arrests rivalled Stalin's. Once he was even sentenced to death - released, ironically, due to an amnesty commemorating the Romanov dynasty. After another detainment, only the 1917 February Revolution in St Petersburg, saved him from a long sentence as political prisoner. When Georgia finally gained its independence (1918-1921) he was arrested again, this time by those he once fought beside - the Social Democratic Mensheviks. They saw him as a Russian Bolshevik agent – which he was – dedicated to the removal of the Menshevik government – which he would achieve. Again he was freed, following an agreement between both governments.

But once the Revolution succeeded, Kamo had nothing much left to do – though it didn't dampen his enthusiasm. During the on-going Russian Civil War (1917-1924) he concocted the idea of dressing up as a Russian White Army officer, then mock-attacking a Red Army group. The intention was to lure concealed Whites to reveal their true colours in the fight. Many Party members disagreed, but he prevailed – thus continuing Georgia's rich theatrical tradition into the heart of the Revolution. Eventually of course, the Bolsheviks won the Civil War, thanks almost certainly to similar levels of fanatical devotion.

As for his own demise, after all the daring escapes, murders, shoot-outs and terrorist attacks, Kamo simply fell off his bicycle after being hit by a car on Tbilisi's Elbakidze Street, in 1922. It happened at 10pm in the evening – possibly because as a true Marxist Revolutionary used to concealing identity, he had no lights (though nor did the car...)

He was buried next to the Pushkin bust, close to the place he and his friend Stalin had once robbed the Russian State Bank of around 250,000 roubles. When Georgia regained independence in the 1990s, his grave disappeared – along with many more of the country's historic monuments and architecture. In fact since then, peacetime demolition has been almost as destructive to heritage as that during wartime – a less proud aspect of the national character.

As a final note on Kamo and Georgia's role in the Russian Revolution, we must mention that robbery.

On the 13th of June 1907, at 10am, two open carriages set off from the Russian State Bank (now the Georgian National Bank) at the corner of Sololaki (now Leonidze) Street. They travelled into Yerevan Square (now Freedom Square), along Golovin Avenue (now Rustaveli), past the Caucasian Military HQ, the City Mayor's office, then the Governor's Palace, and the First Classical Gymnasium, heading for the Post Office. Their mission was to pick up some 250,000 Russian roubles, freshly delivered from the mint.

The Bank's Chief Cashier, one Kurdumov and his assistant, sat in one open carriage; the other carried a group of armed Cossacks. Behind them came a squad of Cossack guards on horseback, due to the large amount of money.

But the Revolutionaries had done their homework. They knew about the money's imminent delivery – extracted from bank clerks via the charms of some female Revolutionaries. Its arrival at the Post Office had been announced by a relative of Stalin's first wife, who worked there. The scene was now set for one of the Revolution's most audacious heists – right in the centre of Tbilisi, a stone's throw from the Governor's Palace. It is said even Lenin himself was in on the operation, due to the amount of money to be 'liberated' for the cause.

After Kurdumov picked up the banknotes at the Post Office, he climbed into the carriage and placed the large sealed bag on his knees. The carriages headed back to the bank. But at the corner of Leonidze street, the convoy was suddenly met by a hail of bombs being lobbed from several directions. The explosions, shooting, screams, lasted a good three or four minutes. One carriage flipped over. Soon bodies of Cossacks and horses were lying in Tbilisi's adjoining Yerevan Square. Meanwhile the horses of Kurdumov's carriage panicked, rushed away up Leonidze street. But another Revolutionary tossed a grenade at their legs. The horses crashed to the ground and the carriage spilled Kurdumov and the money onto the street. When the smoke cleared, Kurdumov sat up to find himself miraculously intact; but the bag of money gone. It is said up to 40 people died during the attack - though this is probably an exaggeration.

So who was responsible for the carnage? Popular folk law has it that Joseph Jugashvili, (Stalin, then using his code-name Koba) was the mastermind. It's said he even lobbed a bomb, though others claim at the time he had bandages on his face from being recently beaten up - so wouldn't have ventured onto the streets.

But there's no doubt at all about the attack's prime operative - Kamo. Wearing his Russian officer disguise, he made off with the money up Leonidze Street, having previously positioned a number of agents along the route, ostensibly to usher the public out of harms way.

After the event every member of the Bolshevik team rapidly hid in pre-arranged safe-house across Tbilisi. The money, it is said, was quickly sewn into the sofa at Tbilisi's Observatory, one of Kamo's secret overnight venues. No one was ever arrested for the heist, although many of those picked up from Yerevan Square area that day, ended up charged with other Revolutionary acts.

When the first wave of police raids subsided, Kamo crammed the money into a suitcase, donned his Georgian nobleman disguise, and using Prince Tsulukidze's passport, travelled north all the way to Finland. On arrival he presented the money to Lenin in person. Not only was it life-blood for the Revolution, it also provided personal income for the Bolshevik Party leaders.

Nor was it the first major robbery in Georgia. Prior to this, 300,000 roubles had been expropriated from the Kvirila railway station, Zestaponi. When added to the other heists, it is said over a million Bolshevik roubles were gathered from Georgia alone.

The majority of Social-Democrats didn't support such violent acts of fund-raising, causing yet more severance between the Mensheviks and Bolsheviks.

The joke was, a good proportion of the money had eventually to be burned, as the police distributed the banknote serial numbers to most European Banks. Anyone trying to exchange them would be arrested on the spot.

And a few were. But again, with that heavy irony that follows every revolution, many found themselves reprieved as part of the Romanov Dynasty's 300th anniversary amnesty. The dynasty they would very soon end for ever with the 1917, October Revolution.

Indeed with that Revolution, all the years of insurrection finally bore fruit – leading to Georgia's proud three years (1918-1921) as the world's first ever Social Democratic (Menshevik) country. So to some extent, the dreams of the Georgian Romantics, nationalists and early outlaws, did find a sort-of reality.

That is, until their former protégées and allies, the Bolsheviks, established another, even more severe, homogenising system of national repression - the USSR.

Chapter 14

The Painter, Nikala

How important is the artist in Georgia?

Extremely, most people say.

Theatre critics, art historians, actors, writers, have all held major political roles in the country's development. And this includes painters. Indeed every Georgian child since the early middle-ages has grown up surrounded by vivid images painted on the church walls – turning imagery and colour into a kind of instinct.

So, a very good time to paint our own portrait of Georgia's most famous and loved artist.

A man of about 45 is walking down a Tbilisi street: tallish, thin, unshaved, wearing a second-hand, blue jacket and wide, black trousers. On his head sits a Russian *kepi*. He goes slowly, a little unsurely, perhaps with a hint of melancholy. Which is how Niko Pirosmani (1862 – 1918) appears to have made his way through the world during his last ten years. A painter known only locally until right at the end of his career - but afterwards celebrated as a national treasure, his work showing in galleries around the world. After he was discovered, they compared him to Henri Rousseau. Pablo Picasso declared himself a fan, creating an etching of Pirosmani as a fine exponent of the Neo-Primitivist or Naïve style. In 2018 one of his paintings fetched GBP2.23 million at Sotheby's in London.

A fact that would have flabbergasted the impoverished artist – who died in complete obscurity, to be buried in a pauper's grave, its location now lost.

Alternatively known as Nikala, Niko Pirosmani, Pirosmanashvili, the Great Piri (after his death), 'the Count,' (behind his back), or just Niko, he became a frequently spotted figure in Tbilisi during one of its greatest periods of change. His wanderings took him along boulevards and alleys, into markets, restaurants, flop-houses as an outsider, who cast a vivid, child-like eye on the city's daily activity. He developed his own unique style of portraiture, painting everyday life in all its facets. Feasts, merchants, children, in-keepers, janitors, organ grinders, singers, shepherds, bears, deer, clothing, again and again – mostly for the price of his next few meals, or a bed for the night. But his beautifully stark, high-contrast images seemed to charm everyone, rich and poor, both then and now. Today some say they provide Georgia's richest set of snapshots of early 20th century Tiflis life.

As outsider-artists go, he inhabited the fringes of hoboism, but with enough business sense to fix on a single career. As for his character; afflicted by a terrible modesty that rarely demanded more than subsistence payment for his work, though not quite enough to stop him knocking on doors for commissions when the wolf banged his own. His stamping ground was mostly the Asian, poorer section of the city. So it's worth making a brief distinction between Tbilisi's old and new towns.

The boundary that Niko rarely crossed, lay along the so-called Middle Bazaar, roughly today's Kote Abkhazi (former Lesilidze) Street. The kinds of art encountered there depended on whether the artist worked its upper or lower sections. In the upper part, built by the Russians, artists tended to be educated with solid academic backgrounds. New city men.

In the lower, painters were usually poorly educated, in Niko's case learning to write mostly from the necessity of painting shop signs and words without mistakes. But beyond the world of words, a man with an instinctive understanding of shape and colour, also enough practicality to learn how to render it efficiently onto tin or cardboard. Indeed it was this raw, untutored aesthetic that the Russian, and later European avant-garde, like the Futurist writer and artist Ilia Zdanevich (1894-1975 – author of *Rapture*), found so refreshing and promoted in a Moscow exhibition in 1913. The process that gradually elevated Niko to his posthumous stardom.

His commissions were varied – from shop and tavern sign-work, to murals, to elaborately written death announcements. To each he gave his own colour and flare, but in lean times he could also take jobs as a regular house-painter.

The businesses and individuals he served represented a good section of the newly prospering capital city. After a thousand years of not much going on, Tbilisi was suddenly leaping forward into the 20th century, riding a tidal-wave of oil wealth from Baku. It had entered the stage where houses and shop-fronts required beautification. Art-Nouveau was reaching its zenith, and hardly a week passed without a new shop, tavern or entertainment venue. All required the artistic touch, outside and in; self-taught or not.

And Niko wasn't alone. A number of other self-educated artists were entering the new profession. One was Gigo Zaziashvili's (1868-1952), and early-on the two artists briefly shared a studio. Then later, at the end of Niko's life, Gigo helped Niko simply to survive.

Encouraged not by school or training, but his dressmaker father, it would be Gigo's father's high blood pressure that led to his son's artistic career. Having received the usual blood-letting treatment from a local barber - less blood, less pressure, so they believed – his father's arm became infected; not helped by an ongoing passion for boxing. Before long it required amputation. Thus, the newly one-armed dressmaker had to change profession - to night-watchman. It was during the endless hours of nothing that he took up drawing. Soon this would become a passion equal to boxing – which he then passed onto his son. Thus Gigo entered the new profession without any guild or traditional training – like Niko. He became one of a community of artists who shared the hard-to-find paints and materials – while still competing with each other for commissions.

Niko Pirosmani's success may have come from the fact he rarely charged money for his paintings. His shyness meant he saw his work as a means to stay alive, rather than an investment into any long-term future. Life in a kind of eternal present-tense in which he found places to sleep mostly ad hoc and for free. But although with no house or studio to maintain, only paints to buy or make, and a relatively full order book - he still remained almost permanently penniless.

It was the number of his commissions that might explain his paintings presence today, as compared to those of other forgotten artists of the time. And still only a fifth of his pictures are thought to have survived. His main area for commissions centred around the railway station area and Rikhe on the right-hand bank of the Mtkvari - then a major residential district (since eradicated by the Soviets). He always faithfully carried out instructions and worked fast.

Top image - *Tatar and Camel by Pirosmani*
Lower image - *the artist from one of his few photos*

CHAPTER 14

Vano Abaev, an Ossetian owner of a small hotel in the Yarmuka district (near Sioni Cathedral), often invited Pirosmani to create murals on his interior walls – then the new fashion. Especially attractive when the cost was hardly more than that of a regular house-painter. The hotelier was also a friend of Vazha Pshavela, and it was in this hotel that Pirosmani met the famous poet. The artist had been greatly impressed with Vazha's children's fable, *The Fawn's Story*, so promptly painted a powerful rendition of the dying young deer in the tavern dining-room. Perhaps this gives a clue to Niko's outsider's sensibility, for the owner promptly demanded its removal from the eating venue. Without a word of complaint, Pirosmani obliged; painting it over with his *Noblemen's Feast*.

His commissions were usually very specific. A customer might request a picture of himself holding a wine horn in one hand, a champion ram on a chain in the other – quite probably because he didn't have one. Thus Niko maintained the artist's traditional role of compensating for clients' ambitions.

Some taverns would have murals painted on virtually every wall – so many they occasionally ran out of ideas. In which case Niko would head out onto the street, spot an everyday scene, then return and paint it from memory – like a simple cart covered with a tent, or a Silk Road trader with his camel. Some might call this quotidian or uninspired; but under Pirosmani's primary-coloured touch, it could never be. The simplicity of his brush-strokes, use of rich colouring, emphasis of unexpected detail, provided everyday sights with an internal glow that other artists rarely achieved. His images, although childlike, always told a story, like his portrayal of a camel owner, attached by a tiny string to the large, imperious animal. It inevitably begs the question - who controlled who?

Often he wouldn't only paint the commissioned work. If someone was generous in his barter system of payment – not only providing plenty of food and *araki*, (home-made Georgian vodka), but also a place to sleep, he'd do extra paintings, even portraits. Mostly he used oil paint and developed his own personal techniques, like using a mixture of soot and lime for background, and painting on plush leatherette – normally used for carriage-seat upholstery. Wherever possible he'd use good quality paints which he mixed on a plate, provided, he insisted, by the tavern owner.

By then Tbilisi had a couple of shops that sold expensive English paints. Niko was a regular customer in one, until it closed at the start of WWI. It allowed him to work on many surfaces, including tin or glass. His low prices were widely known, though he occasionally did receive a few of the necessary roubles.

As for Pirosmani's self-presentation - not what you'd expect of a Lower City member. He liked to cast a veneer of elegance over his impoverishment and always chose his second-hand clothes carefully. It earned him the nickname of 'the Count' among tavern owners. A man always dapper in appearance, yet happy enough to accept a pair of used shoes as payment for his work – then apologise for not presenting himself as properly dressed.

Another unusual trait of character was his punctual debt-repayment. When the Artists' Association gave him a grant of ten roubles, he hated the feeling of indebtedness, so promptly presented them back with a large painting.

But behind his pennilessness lay another character trait. Pirosmani was an alcoholic - known not to be able to paint without a drink to hand. He'd sip from a glass most of the day, and for years on end. It weakened his immune system and some say led to his early death in 1918, succumbing, almost certainly to the then raging Spanish Flu.

He'd start drinking early in the morning, often to the sound of the tavern barrel-organs' jaunty tunes, announcing opening-time and luring in the day's fresh set of customers. Although always avoiding joining the clientele – he disliked noisy groups - he'd never refuse an offered glass and by the day's end was usually contentedly drunk. As one of his friends put it, he painted to get drunk, then drank to paint, while always trying to look dignified.

But in his earlier years Pirosmani had a very different, more sober life. Once he tried running a small shop. When that didn't work, he switched to a roadside tavern. After that failure he briefly took the job of railway conductor. But his heart wasn't there either - already knowing its true calling. This period of his life was featured in Giorgi Shengelaia's very popular, prize-winning film 'Pirosmani' (1969).

They say it was when he visited Tbilisi's Ortachala Gardens and saw a French singer called Margarita, that he immediately fell in love. He then temporally ruined himself by buying her flowers, and painting the famous portrait of her that today would buy a chain of flower shops. But in the end that type of love wasn't for Niko – more the bottle-shaped kind and with it, a single life.

Niko's portrait of his new friend Ilia Zdanevich, who with his brother Kyrill, discovered Pirosmani, to present his work first in Moscow, then internationally.

CHARACTER in Georgia

With no home or workshop, he'd sometimes hide himself away in craftsman's shops, or the room of the poet Davit Givishvili, in Avlabari. The two could sit for hours, chatting, leafing through books, waiting for work to arrive – usually, in Niko's case, from a tavern owner.

And it's worth saying a word about those Tbilisi publicans. Tough, hard-working, often of peasant-stock recently arriving in the city, trying on a new business. Their motivations were many, and not all concerned with the bottom-line. Some started out as *karachokheli* (nomad street craftsmen, members of the *Hamkari* guild); others thieves; some *pirali* trying to make good. Thus they had a good eye for human character, particularly criminals – who they'd either shelter or eject quickly out onto the street. But they always welcomed Niko as one of their gentler, more gracious customers.

One such publican known as Black Vano, always ordered his dairy products from the Molokans – a Slavonic Christian sect, treated as heretics by Russian Orthodoxy. Their name derives from their consumption of dairy, or *moloko* – milk, during fasts. They, among several other sects, had taken refuge for centuries in Georgia. It lasted until the 1990s, when political unrest and economic conditions forced them to return north. Vano admired the Molokan's reputation for honesty and hard work, so commissioned a painting from Pirosmani. Wearing blue or pink satin shirts with black waistcoats, long, well-groomed beards, polished tall boots – the picture is a fine record of one of Georgia's lost ethnic groups.

In truth, many business owners literally took care of Nikala. They gave him a roof and work, then fed him. No one knows exactly how many pictures he made during his life – just a lot. Much of his time he spent on the move. When asked where he lived, he'd merely point east or west saying, 'just some room across the river.'

His portraits were mostly of people he knew, or friends. One of his more famous portraits - that critics later named *The Janitor* - shows his close friend Rashid Almoev, the Yazidi caretaker of Mirzoev's caravanserai in Rikhe. Another small room inhabitant.

Nikala also gained a reputation for sudden and passionate beliefs. During the First Russian Revolution he took to promoting the Menshevik cause, creating many uncommissioned 'Down with the Tsar!' posters, placing or painting them graffiti-style on tavern doors/walls. For the most part the owners let him – that is until the police arrived, demanding their removal/overpainting.

Which left Niko reverting to more subtle tactics. Every year the various Tbilisi guilds would hold festivals - colourful parades replete with music and banners illustrating and coinciding with the Saint-day of their particular profession. Part of their purpose was to host the guild-initiations for new members – which involved being blessed by a priest then slapped across the face by the guild-master. Only after this ancient ritual was completed could the feast begin - usually in a *dukani* ('tavern') or the Ortachala Gardens. Always a good money-spinner for the hospitality business, and tavern owners commissioned large placards to illustrate the various guilds, decorated with their specific symbols, often including the members themselves, carefully lined up according to rank.

Traditionally the banners had a blue background, but the Revolution-supporting Nikala, made them red – the colour of Revolution. Not everyone spotted the allusion, but the police, of course, did. To some considerable embarrassment, the owners were then forced to scratch off the offensive colour, repainting it blue.

When the new Mukhraini Bridge was completed in 1911, it triggered the rapid development of the Rikhe district on the left bank, with rows of houses eventually reaching the Metekhi Bridge. One in particular stood out from the others. A narrow, passage-like building with wide first floor balcony overlooking the river - giving it an unusual, weightless appearance. This would become the Asatiani Tea House, popular for its coolness in summer and superb river views.

Some said it reminded them of a plane wing – so the owner made a bold marketing decision, trying to brand-link his building with Georgia's first ever pilot, Besarion Keburia. The dashing aviator, famous for his aerial displays over Didube and Vake (then safely uninhabited, flat areas), was admired by the whole city. Rich and poor alike gazed in fascination up into the air; some on the east bank even wrote poems about him. One such verse went,

> '*Fearless and free*
> *Besarion Keburia*

crosses the Mtkvari
without a bridge
then climbs the sky
without a ladder.'

The Tea House owner, Mr Asatiani, then commissioned new work from Pirosmani – three murals and a sign. One mural was a simple portrait of Keburia. The second on the facing wall, should have been a landscape, but due to the building's narrowness, Nika inscribed the poem instead. When completed, Keburia was invited to the grand unveiling, and was much surprised by the poem, which he'd never heard. A fact revealing just how separate the European and Asian sections of the city had become.

But the event brought a rare moment of fame for Nika. Though it would take until the beginning of WWI for his reputation to move uptown.

One interesting fact about Pirosmani's work was that although his pictures, murals and signs adorned hundreds of shops, inns, taverns, restaurants, tea and coffee houses in the Lower City, very few of the educated Upper City citizens ever saw them – save perhaps around the railway station.

And it was here, in one of the Station Square inns, that three very important visitors to Tbilisi, spotted his work for the first time. The two Zdanevich brothers, Kyrill and Ilia, and their friend, the 'Rayonist' artist, Michel LeDantiu – founder of the *Bloodless Murder* magazine. For them a moment of grand discovery – which should have ushered in a completely new era for Nikala's career. But strangely, it changed very little in his few remaining years.

Arriving in Tbilisi on holiday, the three Moscow-based Futurists had come to hunt down local ceramics, but were instantly captivated by Pirosmani's Primitivist style work. They began scouring inns and taverns, assiduously collecting his pictures.

Finally they met Pirosmani himself: dressed in his usual smart black jacket, finishing the sign for a dairy shop. The four artists talked and quickly became friends. Pirosmani then painted for them – including a portrait of Ilia Zdanevich, who was half-Georgian - giving the pictures away as gifts. They also purchased others off the walls of shop and tavern owners, who, glad for the money, knew they could re-hire Pirosmani and replace them at a fraction the cost. During one of these purchasing expeditions, LeDantiu ended up alone at Black Vano's inn. He began taking notes on the pictures, but to Vano he looked exactly like a spy for the *Okhrana* - gathering information on his Revolutionary customers. A fight ensued, but the *Bloodless Murder,* editor acquitted himself well, and next day the Zdanevich brothers returned to apologise, finding Black Vano nursing the Rayonist gift of a swollen black eye.

After their holiday the three Futurists returned to Russia promoting the pictures, both there and later in Europe. They also tried to convince Tbilisi's Academia of Pirosmani's highly original talent. But none would, or could see it – that is until after his death.

Their trip to Tbilisi would be blissfully remote from the imminent World War, in which LeDantiu would lose his life and Ilia Zdanevich, very nearly.

When the First World War began, many of Tbilisi's shops and taverns had to close. The city even underwent a brief period of prohibition, directly impacting on Nikala. The capital soon transformed into a collection-point for Russian soldiers escaping the Turkish war, many exchanging boots and coats for any alcohol they could source in the wine-rich nation. Niko among them.

The person who probably did more for Pirosmani than any other in his life, was his old friend Gigo Zaziashvili, who'd learnt to paint from his one-armed father, then shared a studio with Niko. Over the years, thanks to hard graft, he'd evolved into a talented icon painter, then in high demand. He owned a grand studio on the border of the Upper and Lower city and was friendly with many of the city's elite artists.

During Nika's last four years of life, Zaziashvili scooped him up off the street, drunk and hungry many times; took him to his studio, helped him find work.

Some have said that once he witnessed the painter's wealth, Pirosmani became envious of Zaziashvili's success. But that cannot be true, for Nikala inhabited an entirely different world to Gigo, with not the remotest interest in any such regular, organised life.

Around that time, a wealthy wine merchant commissioned a portrait of himself from Pirosmani. But not happy with Niko's Primitivist rendition, he asked Zaziashvili to re-do it, clearly preferring the more photographic realism of the icon painter. Zaziashvili agreed to 'fix' the painting, but lamented he could never fix Niko's lifestyle. He tried many times, even introduced him to the Upper City artists. Twice they helped the impoverished artist by collecting and giving him money. On both occasions Lado Gudiashvili (1896-1980), who later became a famous painter himself, was charged to hunt Niko down and deliver the cash. The first time he succeeded, but the second in 1918, the year Nikala died, he failed.

His physical decline started in 1916. By then he'd met the city's artistic elite. Some even professed to like his work. He featured twice in local newspapers. The first article included his photo, proclaiming him a new talent. In normal circumstances this meant official recognition and the mark of success. Papers were then trusted – unlike in the subsequent Communist years when praise in the press – by then all official - meant toadying to the regime.

But the second article proved devastating for Niko. It carried a caricature of a barefoot, unshaven Pirosmani, painting his famous spotted giraffe (made solely from someone's description, for he'd never seen one), with the well-known writer Grigol Robakidze (1880-1962) standing behind, advising him to study for another 20 years to become 'a real artist,' worthy of an exhibition. Zaziashvili's wife remembers a highly agitated Nikala telling her husband that, 'since you arranged my meeting with the artists, now *you* must protect me from them!'

Just as in the directness of his paintings, Niko took the joke completely to heart, failing to catch any hint of irony. Along with many outsider artists (and children), he experienced irony as a form of lying. He even remarked that he'd be dead in 20 years, so wouldn't live to see his exhibition.

He was absolutely right and shortly vanished totally, back into the Lower City.

At the time the streets were filled with walking-wounded from the Turkish war. The Battle of Erzurum had recently been won by Russia, and hospitals were full. Furthermore it wouldn't take long for the Spanish Flu to arrive. Eventually Zaziashvili decided to hunt down Pirosmani and found him drinking with coachmen next to the Molokans' market. Zaziashvili tried to persuade Niko to return to the Upper City, show his face to the high-brow artists, prove himself above their lampooning. But Pirosmani replied, he'd only be drinking with his true friends from now on.

The infamous cartoon satirising Niko Pirosmani (in bare feet painting his giraffe) being lectured by the writer Grigol Robakidze

This was the time he found new lodgings in a storage space under some warehouse stairs, among the firewood. The owner was Archil Maisuradze, a one-legged cobbler, who took care of the now increasingly sick artist, even arranging commissions for him in a nearby hotel.

Meanwhile the Spanish Flu began its deadly march across Europe, killing rich and poor alike, defying every medicine. When Pirosmani didn't turn up for work three days in a row, Maisuradze returned to the wood-locker to find him lying under the stairs, already at death's door. Although poor himself, he paid for a doctor, then a carriage to take Pirosmani to hospital. But Niko died the next day, on Easter Sunday.

As a final note we might mention a young man nicknamed Short Misha, who'd worked in the shop where Pirosmani once bought his paints. After the shop went out of business, Misha found employment transporting the city's many untended dead – mostly tramps, soldiers, flu victims. The state had been forced to create a special new cemetery, the

Peter and Paul, where they were quickly buried for the sake of sanitation, usually without priest or ritual.

Misha recognised Pirosmani's body while transporting it. En-route to the cemetery he encountered another man, Vaso, who also knew Pirosmani. The two of them managed to find a priest and give Niko a summary Christian burial.

Shortly afterwards a few of Nikala's friends returned to toast his memory at the graveside, pouring wine on the ground as is the Georgia custom - like the parting gift to one who'd loved it so much. One of them, Shasho, the cap-maker, then commissioned a gravestone, but it has since vanished.

It was only after his death that Pirosmani's popularity began to soar, both home and abroad. Suddenly Georgian writers and artists were lining up to publish their memories of the brilliant Primitivist, eagerly buying his paintings, seeking out those who'd known him. As for Gigo Zaziashvili, the one who knew and cared-for Niko the most, he remained distinctly cool to the people swarming around the international artist's reputation, buttering up their stories and memories about this highly original, shy Georgian artist.

Indeed on his own death bed in 1952, Gigo recalled his sadness at being in Kakheti, not knowing about Niko's tragic final days, trapped under those warehouse stairs. He said, had he been in Tbilisi then, he would have done what they never did, found and looked after the man who would become - though nobody knew it then - Georgia's most beloved and celebrated artist of all time.

Chapter 15

Independence - and then the Bolsheviks

As said previously, the 26th May 1918 was a huge moment for the Georgian nation. Some even claim the country's entire history aimed toward that single moment - when the bell of independence rang out from St David's church, above Tbilisi. The Gurian, Noe Ramishvili had just signed the Declaration of Independence, to become Chairman of the Provisional Government of the new Democratic Republic of Georgia.

Ahead lay a historic three years when the world's first Menshevik government, under the leadership of Noe Jordania (who shortly took over from Ramishvili), set out to create a truly modern democracy, guided by its own unique Constitution. It led to many changes in daily life, redistribution of wealth and lands (mostly from nobility to peasants), discussions and arguments, to the degree that sometimes it was hard to know who wanted what from the new country.

But the proudly created Georgian State battled forward, one must say, in most difficult circumstances. Soon it had a State University, founded in January 1918, in the building of the former Georgian Nobility Gymnasium - the first of its kind in the Caucasus (designed by the Georgian Simon Kldiashvili). It introduced an eight-hour work day and full democracy with universal suffrage – ahead even of America. In the 1919 democratic election, the Mensheviks received 80% of the vote, conclusively proving their popularity. This was far more than in either Armenia or Azerbaijan, which also enjoyed brief periods of independence. One reason for their success, as compared to the increasingly jealous Bolsheviks, was the diversity of their leadership - composed of workers, businessmen, lawyers, former nobles, graduates of the religious seminaries, and women. In fact Georgia could soon boast the world's first elected, female, Muslim member of a Regional Council. Her name was Peri-Khan Sofiyeva and she took her position in the village of Karajala – about 20km east of Tbilisi. Although losing her position with the arrival of the Bolsheviks, (the party declaring themselves the great equaliser of the sexes), she lived on into the 1950s, unlike so many of her male co-electees - who ended up shot, mostly in the 1930s.

The Mensheviks, who then called themselves the Georgian Social Democratic Workers Party - didn't insist on immediate nationalisation of all industries, like the Bolsheviks. The transition from being a Russian colony to its own, dignified socialist state, would be along a multi-partied, hotly discussed, heroically bumpy road.

As for those who'd nobly pulled Georgia forward to this point... The two individuals most yearning to witness the birth of the new nation - Akaki Tsereteli and Vazha Pshavela - never would. Both died in 1915. That year's terrible heat took Vazha in the summer, when his stomach illness returned. The final straw came as his confinement in Tbilisi, far away from the fresh air and cool water of his mountains. His regime of watermelons and sipped red wine eventually failed. When he knew he was dying, he asked to be carried to a field, just so he could lie feeling the grass on his cheeks – but never was. Instead his numerous fans continued to fête him with endless bouquets of flowers, particularly violets.

After a week in hospital he died. He was laid out in Kashveti church, to then be buried in Didube cemetery. Many years later Lavrenti Beria, as First Secretary of the Georgian Soviet Socialist Republic (SSR), moved him to the poets' pantheon at St David's Church, above Mtatsminda.

Among the many speeches and words of veneration at his funeral, one wreath stood out from the others bearing the simple inscription;

'To Vazha Pshavela from Georgia.' He would have wished for nothing more.

As for Akaki, he died in his family home in Skhvitori, in Upper Imereti, which today houses an excellent museum. His funeral became an epic event. He was carried town to town, all the way to St David's church in Tbilisi's Mtatsminda. As he passed, thousands of people came out to watch and express their appreciation. Many would deliver impassioned speeches from balconies - praising one of Georgia's most popular-ever poets. Some even recalled Akaki's joke about funerals when he said, 'if any of you feel like buying me a bouquet when I die, could you just give me the money now.'

CHAPTER 15

Meanwhile the entirely new, all-Georgian government, did its best to fulfil the promises made to its now Socialist population.

Their most significant reform was land. The Agrarian Reform Law was passed in January 1919, nationalising all the oversized private estates. Many nobility, some say the majority, were happy to give up good sections of their property to the peasants. Word was sent out by the new government that estates would be offered for sale at very low prices to locals – as equally as possible – turning peasants into landowners themselves. The original owners, nearly always nobility, were allowed to keep a small portion of their former estates and work the fields themselves. For the most part, particularly in Western Georgia, the nobles went along with this arrangement; some even enthusiastically.

'This is the payment we make for freedom,' ran the slogan.

Indeed even as early as 1911, one Revolutionary from the Kartli nobility – Rezo Gabashvili (although not a Menshevik and harsh critic of Jordania) bought, then gave away some 5000 hectares of land across Georgia, to the local peasantry.

But in Eastern and Southern Georgia, some resisted. The largest landowner in the Akhaltsikhe region, the Muslim prince, Server Bek Jakeli – (called Koblianski by the Russians after his village's name), was furious at this shattering of a centuries-old tradition. When the local Committee declared his large apple orchards now property of the state, he refused to hand them over. He said he'd rather offer them to the Ottomans – Georgia's traditional enemies – than let them be snatched by any fanatic Socialists. He'd already formed a pan-Muslim movement in Southern Georgia. Now he armed his supporters and instructed them to defend his territory down to the last square metre. In response the Tbilisi government sent down a large military contingent which quickly defeated Bek's rebels, forcing him to flee across the border to Istanbul, where he lived on until 1962.

But one fact couldn't be avoided; the new Menshevik government had landed into a sea of political chaos – mostly not of its own making. The First World War had just ended; the German military who until then were the guardians of Georgia, soon fled. They were replaced by a rather unsympathetic British garrison of some 20,000 troops. Meanwhile the Armenians, south of the border, seeing an opportunity to regain what they saw as their former territories, suddenly invaded. They advanced to within 50 kilometres of Tbilisi before being pushed back in a counter attack. The British then instructed the Georgians not to pursue them on into the Lori region, meaning that today Lori remains in Armenia.

Then with impeccable timing came the 1920 earthquake in Gori - 8.0 on the Richter scale, killing 145 people, heavily damaging the castle, many churches and 750 other buildings. A further contribution to the instability surrounding the new government, this time from nature.

The harsh realities of the new Republic were well summed up by one of Kutaisi's more popular social commentators, Sergia Eristavi. Someone rushed up to him saying, 'Isn't it wonderful, the French have recognised us!' This referred to the fact that the French government had just declared The Democratic Republic of Georgia a bone-fide nation in its own right. Sergia, then standing on the city's Chain Bridge, glanced down at the rapidly flowing Rioni river replying, 'Yes it is wonderful, especially when you're drowning, shouting out 'help me!' and someone just waves back and says 'It's OK, I recognise you, Sergia!'

As part of their technique to cleanse themselves from the stain of Tsarist influence, the Mensheviks created their own currency. They announced the replacement of the Russian Imperial rouble with their own '*maneti*' - a paper currency whose first and lowest denomination was a one *kopek* note. Because they had no financial experience they printed their new, beautifully designed currency, way too freely. This led to inflation on a massive scale. Soon the *maneti* turned into the 'Bon' (a reference to 'bond') and they were printing 5,000 Bon notes. By 1923 the new Bolshevik government, which took over the currency and translated it to a trans-Caucasian rouble, was printing 100,000,000 rouble notes – which had only slightly more value than the original kopeks. People joked that train journeys were becoming increasingly difficult, because locals needed to carry so much currency to market, they'd no room to sit anymore. Some tried to use the old Russian silver coins where they could, but they became increasingly scarce. The Russian Poet Osip Mandlestam, in his poetic travelogue *Journey to Armenia,* described waking each morning in Batumi to the sound of the currency dealers announcing the new, decreased value of the Georgian currency, as a kind of birdsong.

Upper: *a fifty kopek note from the Democratic Republic of Georgia (1918-21)*
Lower: *a hundred million rouble note from 1924, early Bolshevik era.*

As for daily life in the towns and villages, periodic food shortages continued. There might be no bread on Tuesday, eggs on Wednesday, long queues for kerosene on Thursday. But being Georgia, wine was always plentiful. In the remoter, poor regions and villages there could still be robberies, even local Communist rebellions, leading to endless arguments in local Committees. But no starvation and most importantly, people remained, for the most part, optimistic for their new country.

To announce their new liberation to the world, the Mensheviks renamed Tbilisi's central square, Freedom Square. This lasted until 1922 when the Bolsheviks re-titled it *Zak Federatia Moidani* (Trans Caucasian Federation Square). It remained this way until 1940 when it adopted the name of Georgia's Communist leader, Beria, to be replaced after his death in 1953, by Comrade 'Lenin' – until 1990, when it became Freedom Square again.

CHARACTER in Georgia

As a side note one might mention in 1936, Beria, the First Secretary of the Georgian SSR (Soviet Socialist Republic), officially changed the name of Tbilisi from Tplisis (old Georgian version of '*tpili*' – 'warm'), to Tbilisi, making it easier to pronounce. Until then the Russians always used the Turkish/Persian name, Tiflis. But with the new, simpler pronunciation, they started to use the correct name.

As for the positive side of the social changes, these quietly continued across the country. Georgians quickly began doing again what they did best, inviting visitors in with welcoming arms. Indeed Tbilisi soon became a very bohemian city, especially friendly to artists. The Mensheviks, after suffering years of having to disguise the meaning of their words in articles, public speeches, conversations - removed all censorship. The media became completely free. They even supported the start of the first Writer's Union, ostensibly to give writers an independent voice. Ironically, the Bolsheviks would keep it on, using the membership list as a device to keep an eye on all words, as they enforced an even worse regime of censorship than the Tsarist *Okhrana* – via their own secret police, the *Cheka*.

Tbilisi attracted artists from all over Europe. Ilia Zdanevich returned and founded *41 Degrees*, the Futurist movement in Tbilisi (41 degrees indicates high temperature). In those heady days you might easily walk past a Futurist on Rustaveli Avenue, wearing his coat upside down. Or encounter gallery invasions by activists shouting, 'Art is Dead!' 'Speed is Beauty,' 'Museums are Graveyards!'

The atmosphere was extremely free, wildly creative – an 'exciting time to live' visitors said. The *Blue Horns* literary movement - started in 1915 Kutaisi – flourished, along with their magazines like *Dreaming Ibex*. Inside the Kimerioni Cafe on Rustaveli Avenue (under today's Rustaveli theatre) coffee drinkers might see artists like Ziga Polishevsky, Serge Sudeikin, Lado Gudiashvili, who along with David Kakabadze, painted its murals. They might hear spontaneous recitals from poets Paolo Iashvili, Tisian Tabidze, Elena Dariani, Sandro Euli, or the Russians, Osip Mandlestam, Sergei Yesenin – until the Bolshevik invasion of 1921.

We might also mention the artist Lado Gudiashvili, who watched all the changes in Georgia from the other end of a paint brush; starting at the turn of the 20th century, right through to the 1970s. A humble man who painted the dancers on the Kimerioni wall in 1919, then pilgrimaged over to Paris to hang out with the international art-world stars. But interestingly he returned to Tbilisi in 1926 shortly after the terrible repressions of 1924, following the failed Menshevik insurrection against the Bolsheviks.

Initially the Communists still paid artists a stipend. Whether he received this or no, isn't sure. But either way that wasn't the reason. His fellow artists, David Kakabadze, Ketevan Margalashvili, and Elene Akvlediani had all been doing well in Paris's Latin Quarter, but felt the need to return home - as if their homeland was a key component of their careers. Was it that same homesickness experienced by so many Georgians abroad, then and now? One so well alluded to in Nikoloz Baratashvili's poem *Merani* when he asks the galloping horse to;

> *'fly me over the borders of fate*
> *and leave behind all life's most precious things*
> *like burial in one's homeland grave'*

Constructivist book cover for the Bolshevik poet, Sandro Euli's 'Triumphant Factory.' By 1923 only Bolsheviks or sympathisers would be making it into print. Note the old spelling of Tbilisi as 'Tpilisi,' bottom right and the explosive design, echoing the ongoing Revolutionary war in Russia.

CHARACTER in Georgia

Gudiashvili would remain back in Tbilisi for the rest of his life, living in two rooms, being supported by his wife, not having a personal exhibition for 40 years. But he never tried to leave.

Home is clearly another key ingredient in the national character.

The atmosphere of Menshevik freedom also drew participants from other hard-pressed communities, like mystical religious sects or cults. Giorgi Gurdjieff, author of *Meetings with Remarkable Men,* found himself drawn back to Tbilisi, after spending some of his youth there. He created his 'Institute for the Harmonious Human Development of Man' in 1919 somewhere in Avlabari; and began to attract followers. His teachings borrowed from Caucasian Sufi traditions, like Rindi - which had once inspired Lasha Giorgi, Queen Tamar's son in the 12th century. Some also say that the free-spirited *kharachokheli* Tbilisi craftsmen, also carried some of the tradition in their poetic approach to life. Gurdjieff was particularly attracted to dance, then undergoing a renaissance in Georgia. The father of George Balanchine (co-founder of the New York City Ballet), Meliton, was briefly Minister of Culture in the new Menshevik government. Gurdjieff also employed some of the Tibetan Buddhist techniques for suppressing the self. Very different from those soon to be used by the Communists, who demanded self-sacrifice on behalf of the dictatorship of the proletariat. With the gathering threat of Communist repression, Gurdjieff had to rapidly abandon his Institute as the Bolsheviks set their very self-centred eyes on a conquest of Georgia.

However before they arrived, in September 1920 a multi-national group of leading Social Democrats made a historic visit to Georgia on a similar mission - to witness and briefly enjoy the open, tolerant atmosphere of Menshevik Georgia. They were led by Karl Kautsky (1854-1938), then the effective Social Democratic Patriarch (thanks to his long white beard). Among their number were two future heads of state, the Belgian Camille Huysmans (1871-1968) and Ramsay McDonald (1866-1937), the first ever Labour Prime Minister of the United Kingdom in 1924. They were greeted rapturously everywhere by the newly Social Democratic population. Crowds would meet their train delivering stirring, polyphonic renditions of the Internationale, throwing red roses over the oriental carpets spread across the platforms and waiting rooms.

After they returned to their various countries, most presented favourable reports about what they saw in Georgia, and its new Social

Democratic leadership. One point perhaps that they missed in their short visit, was a certain political naivety in the Menshevik leader Noe Jordania. Maybe Lenin had spotted it earlier, shortly after the Social Democrats split in half at the start of the 20th century. Apparently he took Jordania aside saying, 'why are you Georgians interfering with our Russian questions? Better that you just stick to your own.'

While some say this is what Jordania did par-excellence, by creating a Social Democratic country; the harsh double-standard underlying Lenin's comment would come back to haunt him. The openness of Jordania's Menshevik regime also permitted the small number of Georgian Bolsheviks complete freedom for their campaigning. Thus they started their own newspaper, *Communisti* (which continued until 1991), and generally built the internal structure of a fifth column in Tbilisi, ready to greet the Bolshevik army, already gathering in Azerbaijan, Armenia and Sochi district.

The message they spread was effectively;

'All is good. One Socialist party will go, another arrive – so much the better for independent Georgia!'

But of course the Reds were simply preparing to make good Lenin's double standard – for he had every intention of interfering with Georgia – by in fact, wiping the country and its independent culture off the map. Indeed many say that Lenin deliberately set out to strip all the romanticism out of the Revolutionary movement. By replacing it with the dumbing-down simplicity of materialism, he meant to crush all thoughts of personal, or national identity. In reality of course, it would be substituted by an even more strictly defensive, Soviet identity.

At the end of February 1921, just as, ironically, Georgia gained official recognition from the British and American governments, the Bolshevik army suddenly invaded across the Armenian border.

Significantly superior in size to the Georgian defensive forces – who initially put up a stiff resistance – the Bolshevik tanks advanced inexorably. Soon they were threatening Tbilisi. The Menshevik government began gathering papers, money, artefacts and key Georgian symbols, in the event they couldn't stop the Bolsheviks. On the evening of the 24th February, the government headed for the railway station. The waiting train had one carriage reserved for Jordania and his aids; the dining car set aside for documents, cash and Georgian treasures. After several sleepless days,

Jordania decided to take a brief nap, asking his assistant Imnadze to wake him up when the train arrived at Mtskheta. There he intended to disembark, fully expecting to return shortly to Tbilisi.

But Imnadze never woke him, until they reached Gori.

Was this the final sign of the Georgian government's capitulation?

Many felt it was. Jordania looked out the train window in Gori to find the platform brimming with disorientated soldiers, most without officers. Later in his memoirs, General Kvinitadze (1874-1970), leader of the Georgian army wrote that they were deserters. But this only proved how disorganised the army was. Noe Ramishvili, then Georgia's Minister of Internal Affairs, jumped out onto the platform brandishing a shotgun, trying to organise the troops ready for a return to battle. It didn't work. Seeing Jordania in the carriage, seemingly en-route for Kutaisi, if not beyond, all concluded the game was up. Ramishvili eventually climbed back on the train, and it continued west.

On the morning of the 25th of February General Kvinitadze ordered the Georgian army to retreat to Mtskheta and restore the front line. The Red Army drove on into the Georgian capital encountering no resistance. The triumphant Bolsheviks then sent telegrams to the Kremlin saying how the Georgian workers had joyfully greeted the Red Army. That the transfer of power had been as natural as it had been inevitable.

Very quickly Jordania and his parliament abandoned any hope of moving the capital even to Kutaisi. Not long after this, he and the government boarded several ships in Batumi, bound for Italy. On their arrival Mussolini himself assisted the Socialists buy their tickets to France – because he was then a Socialist, though of course not for long.

Jordania would set up the Government in Exile at Leville, near Paris.

Back home, the Menshevik Social Democrats of Georgia had now officially been renamed Bolsheviks.

But most of the former Revolutionaries were not happy - at all. Furthermore many already knew each other from their former joint battles against the Tsar, some were even relatives. Now they found themselves in opposing camps. Some Georgian Marxists who fought against the Red Army, ended up as Red Army officers – to lead very strange double lives. Colonel Rostom Muskhelishvili (1888-1923) who served in the Red Army until 1923, began secretly cooperating with the residue Menshevik soldiers and officers, preparing an uprising against his own Bolsheviks.

The Bolsheviks swarming into the 18th century Cathedral to St David in Kutaisi, in 1923.
First they plundered its contents, then decided to knock it down entirely, replacing
the building with a statue of Lenin. Which they did. They would go on to destroy over a
thousand more churches across Georgia alone.

The rebels had plenty of supporters, as a good number of Georgian politicians and Revolutionaries refused to flee abroad – intending to take back their country. Many turned into guerrillas again – returning to Georgia's forests like *pirali,* tolerating extreme hardships, waiting for the signal. However, unlike in the previous Revolutionary phase, no single organisation existed to effectively manage the insurrection. But the majority of people still wished passionately for the old days, paying lip-service to the increasingly brutal Communist regime – while privately singing songs with words like,

'The Rose will come, the violet will come, and then Jordania will follow,' (in Spring).

But Jordania didn't follow. Instead there were multiple small rebellions – even as early as 1921. They were quickly and severely crushed. Soon the Metekhi prison in Tbilisi was bursting with Menshevik inmates. The *Cheka* proved far more effective than the Tsarist *Okhrana,* and way crueller. For instance in 1923 they executed 93 Metekhi inmates in response to the single murder of a notorious Bolshevik Commissar in Guria (Vazha Pshavela's brother Levan, was one).

Gradually preparations began for the one big uprising. Lacking reliable communications, information exchanges were made via a number of brave individuals, usually travelling by train (to avoid the Red Army road checkpoints, set about every 10 kilometres). They'd then disappear into the forests, search out the guerrilla units, deliver money and instructions, then hurry back to the city.

Once home, disguise was essential. The *Cheka* and its friends were everywhere. The smallest mistake could lead to your downfall – permanently. The young intellectual Dadesh Gelovani (1898-1924) was arrested after his pence-nez fell out of his pocket while stepping out of a *dukhani* (a Georgian tavern). Although dressed like a peasant, the *Cheka* guessed that no worker would own such glasses. It didn't take long for him to be executed.

Because of their omnipresence, the widespread preparations for an uprising didn't escape the *Cheka's* long noses. They employed every trick in the book to squeeze information from detainees and subvert all attempts at dissent – from threats, coercion, torture, to forcibly written fake letters.

CHAPTER 15

The *Cheka* were most effective in eastern Georgia. But in western areas like Guria, with its long history of Revolutionary tactics against the Empire, less so.

Eventually the official uprising was set for the autumn of 1923, then immediately postponed until 1924. Those aware of this continued their everyday life, working the land, avoiding soldiers, waiting for the signal. Meanwhile many prominent activists crept back into Georgia from their Paris immigration.

Insurrection day then changed again; became the 15th or was it, 16th August 1924. Long enough before the grape harvest so as not, hopefully, to spoil it. But when one of the insurrection leaders was arrested on the 6th August, he was horrified to hear his interrogator ask him to confirm the 16th August uprising day. Realising the *Cheka* knew far more than his anti-Soviet Committee believed (established in 1923), he attempted suicide – but failed. However after the rebellion itself failed, the *Cheka* didn't hesitate to complete the job for him. The venue for his execution was a field in Tbilisi's Vake, which then, rather than being a salubrious city district, was mostly scrub-land and a favourite venue for mass execution. Indeed when workers, many years later, came to make Vake Park they ran across many skeletons buried in pits.

But then insurrection day changed again, confusing and frustrating the rebels – to the degree that some even quit the fighting groups.

It became the 20th August, 1924. But not everyone found out. The disjointed groups, scattered across the country, failed not only to act in unison, but often even to communicate. In the mining town of Chiatura, the attack began 24 hours early because the Revolutionary fighters, then hiding in and around the streets, heard gunshots. Thinking this the opening act of the rebellion, they launched their own premature attack – which failed gloriously.

In fact the shooting came from a robbery of the local manganese mine office, carried out by some young, non-political opportunists, intending to time their theft with the chaos of the rebellion. But they too got the date wrong – confirmed when one of the defeated rebels later met a group of young Georgians drying out stolen banknotes on a Turkish beach.

So the 1924 rebellion ended up as a complete failure. Georgia remained in the hands of the Bolsheviks and their offspring until 1990.

Perhaps the last word on Georgia's first heroic period of independence should go to one of its original heroes and formative minds, Ilia Chavchavadze.

'The good thing about the Georgian man is he deals with terrible misfortune and great luck in the same way - with fearlessness and resignation.'

Georgia had to wait seventy more years for its second period of genuine independence as a country. And although it too was also met with civil war in 1991, this time it survived through to the other side, three-quarters intact. And so far it continues on almost in the way that Ilia had intended, though with fingers tightly crossed - as ever.

The Authors

Aka Morchiladze is Georgia's most popular contemporary writer. He has written over 20 novels in Georgian, seven have been translated into German, and two into English. One, *Journey to Karabakh* was made into a film in 2004. He is also creator and host of a highly popular TV program on Georgia's cultural history - which he also teaches at Tbilisi's Ilia State University. Formerly he worked as an official sports correspondent in England, (and still supports Brentford FC). Today he has returned to Georgia to live and write in his family's ancestral region of Lechkumi.

Peter Nasmyth is the author of a number of books on Georgia, including *Georgia in the Mountains of Poetry*, and *Walking in the Caucasus, Georgia.* As a regular visitor to Georgia since 1987, he has made programs for the BBC, exhibitions for the British Council and FCO, been a director of Georgia's first international arts festival, co-founded Prospero's Books, Tbilisi. More recently he co-founded the new 'National Trust of Georgia,' in association with the National Trust of Great Britain's international arm, INTO. He divides his time between the UK and Tbilisi.

ACKNOWLEDGEMENTS

Many thanks to the Writer's House of Georgia for assisting Maya Kiasashvili's translation - without which this book would never have happened. Also a special note to Maya herself for going beyond the call in her work. Tina Mamulashvili from Sulakauri Publishers for making the cogs turn with the new edition. My friend Irakli Topuria for his hundred million rouble note. Julie Christiansen for her patient reading. Orsolya Sárossy from the Tbilisi Opera and her friend Eliso Julakidze who helped supply the good quality Opera Interior illustration. Maia Mania for her constant wisdom and good advice. Marine Mizandari and the team at the National Trust of Georgia for their dedication to Georgia's heritage - that this book celebrates. Maia Kipshidze for the same. To Susanne Channon, Rachel MacPherson, Michael Murphy and all those who gave up time to read through various sections and paragraphs.

COVER PHOTO

Three Caucasian men dressed as chapari fighters from around the turn of the 20th century. Local militia hired by the Empire to fight Revolutionaries and pirali outlaws. Clearly not pirali as they wear medals (bestowed by the Empire). Furthest left is in Gurian dress; the middle wears a Cossack hat and probably is one; the right-hand man is Imeretian - recognisable from his headpiece, rather than hat.

INDEX

215

Old postcard of a Tbilisi market. Top caption reads
Maidani (market square) for carpets and general shopping.
On right side - The Heaven Dukani (restaurant).